Fundamentals of Film Directing

Fundamentals of Film Directing

DAVID K. IRVING

McFarland & Company, Inc., Publishers
Jefferson, North Carolina, and London

LIBRARY OF CONGRESS CATALOGUING-IN-PUBLICATION DATA

Irving, David K.
    Fundamentals of film directing / David K. Irving.
      p.   cm.
    Includes bibliographical references and index.

    ISBN 978-0-7864-4787-9
    softcover : 50# alkaline paper ∞

    1. Motion pictures — Production and direction. I. Title.
PN1995.9.P7174   2010
791.43'0233 — dc22   2009051321

British Library cataloguing data are available

Cover image ©2010 Creations/Shutterstock

Manufactured in the United States of America

McFarland & Company, Inc., Publishers
  Box 611, Jefferson, North Carolina 28640
  www.mcfarlandpub.com

Table of Contents

Preface

A director's mettle is forged on set. The first day that one directs speaks volumes about the path the endeavor will take. Having been on a working set as a film director a half-dozen times I can say with some confidence that the first day's shooting sets a tone for the entire shoot. Directing is a challenging, complicated and exhausting job. It will take less effort if one appreciates and is aware of the ten fundamentals outlined in this book.

Film directing consists of four distinct phases: pre-production, production, post-production and distribution. Pre-production is when all the elements are gathered together; a screenplay is written, financing is secured, artists and craftsmen are hired, and a plan is established for principal photography. Production is when, as Jackie Gleason would say, "And awaaaaay we go!" During post-production the director delivers all the shots taken during principle photography to an editing room to assemble the footage into a cohesive story. Finally, the finished piece forces its way into the marketplace through a distribution network.

Of the four phases, screen writing and editing are crafts a director must understand, appreciate and often execute. Directors may or may not be involved in distribution. Therefore, the key elements suggested in this book emphasize the second phase, production, for it is here that all decisions, focus and momentum fall directly on the shoulders of the director. Here a director cultivates fortitude, the faculty to see a project through against any and all odds, while tenaciously focused on a single vision.

There is no better way to learn about directing than by actually doing it. Books and manuals can serve as a guide. Other films and videos can act as inspiration, and talking about and critiquing films and videos can trigger ideas. However, the two best teachers are failure and success. Experiencing the process of putting a project together, building work muscles, and understanding the craft and discipline of the process are ultimately the best ways to develop your skills.

Any journey begins with a first step. Directing a motion picture starts on the first day of principle photography. The step should be bold, confident and headed in the right direction. All the efforts put into preparation will pay off on this first day. Directing is an exhilarating experience fraught with challenges. The goal of this book is to anticipate and grapple with those challenges.

Introduction

The lights go down. Excitement and anticipation fill the air. Images begin to dance across the silver screen. A little laughter, a few tears. And the house lights come up. The person primarily responsible for this cinematic journey is the film's director. It is possibly one of the greatest jobs on earth.

Cinema should make you forget you are sitting in a theater.
— Roman Polanski

Starting as a popular novelty known as a nickelodeon, cinema blossomed into the incredible art and entertainment form we see today, only one century later. Successfully making the transition from nickelodeons to movie theaters, New York to Los Angeles, black and white to color, silent to sound, film and its small-screen counterpart, television, have become international phenomenon. In both cultural and marketplace arenas, for better or for worse, film and television have made the entire globe a tighter-knit community.

Directing is a multifaceted job. Its description varies from show to show. Certain essentials such as script, cast, crew and budget determine success and failure. By mastering the practical and physical elements of production, while manipulating the psychological landscape, directors improve their chances for success. The ten fundamentals (five physical and five psychological) are the pillars upon which directors build their careers. These elements outline the helpful regulations and rules of procedure established over time by custom.

Many of the director's responsibilities overlap with those of the producer. Much of this book outlines tasks interchangeable between director and producer. Though their job is difficult to define, the producer(s) have a tremendous impact on the final product. The director and the producer must get along, or the production may suffer.

A producer's main focus is the preparation of a picture. Once a film has been written, cast, crewed up and financed, it is turned over to the director. As there may be anywhere from zero to eight producers on any given film, it is difficult to define this position as having only one set of duties. Producing titles range from *executive producer, producer, co-producer, associate producer, assistant producer, line producer* and *executive in charge of production.*

Producing is the art of balancing creative and financial elements that, when merged, produce a picture. In a broad sense, producing requires finding and developing the script, attaching the director and principle actors, securing the financing and selling the picture. There are producers who specialize in screenplay development, financing, production, post-production and sales. Then there are producers who work on several projects at a time. Productions may require a team of producers to pull off a picture. With multiple producers a director needs to be keenly aware of who controls what strings. The only one who can fire a director is the producer.

A strong and creative producer can be a great help to the director. A creative producer understands script, acting and directing. The producer offers the director objectivity when making decisions and gathering information. Some directors produce their own work, but for the most part the producer-director relationship is the first and most important of the many collaborative partnerships a director forges in order to successfully create a film.

A beginning director must master the craft of directing while at the same time exploring and learning about all facets of life, especially those associated with storytelling and human behavior. Veteran director Elia Kazan, in a speech made at Wesleyan University in 1973, stated, "a director must be like a white hunter, construction gang foreman, psychoanalyst, hypnotist, poet, baseball outfielder, bazaar trader, animal trainer, great host and jewel thief." In short, the director has to know everything.

Film as dream, film as music. No art passes our conscience in the way film does, and goes directly to our feelings, deep down into the dark rooms of our souls.
— Ingmar Bergman

In William Goldman's classic 1983 insider's work on the film industry, *Adventures in the Screen Trade*, Mr. Goldman writes extensively on the role of the actor, the producer, the writer, the studio executives and the agent. His chapter dedicated to directors is ostentatiously brief. Only seven words: "Some of my best friends are directors." He adds a three-paragraph postscript to the seven-word chapter that includes some observations about directors. But what is striking is just how indescribable the job is.

The role of individual contributors such as cinematographer, actor, editor, composer, writer, and art director can more easily be defined than a director. The range of director duties swings from all-consuming involvement (consider producer/writer/director/editor/star Buster Keaton) to that of traffic cop (stand here, move there, action, cut, print). The amount of artistry, style and input depends on the talents of the director, the time allotted to direct and an adherence to the ten fundamentals of directing.

Film directing is such an all-encompassing, sometime amorphous, often cryptic, complicated and relatively new vocation, that it is a challenge to be precise about a director's duties. Film directors have been likened to a musical conductor, military general, circus ringmaster, auteur and ship's captain. Each of these established vocations embraces separate attributes important to film directing.

I think cinema, movies, and magic have always been closely associated. The very earliest people who made film were magicians.
— Francis Ford Coppola

Sidney Lumet in his splendid book *Making Movies* equates directing a film to the creation of a mosaic. Each tile (scene) is manufactured. Then these tiles are assembled (edited) to produce a complete picture (film). Tiles are made of clay or stone, paint and glue. The materials a director uses to make a film are the script, actors, camera and sound recorders, art department accouterments, stock and editing machines.

He or she brings to bear all their knowledge and experience about life and human behavior on the project, strikes a creative spark, which then ignites and fuses the components into a whole. After months of polishing, shaping and then carefully placing each tile, the director stands back and views the whole mosaic. He or she should see what the audience sees. And like any work of art, in the end, the whole will hopefully be greater than the sum of its parts.

Every time I go to a movie, it's magic, no matter what the movie's about.

— Steven Spielberg

Screenplay

A director shouldn't get in the way of the movie, the story should.
— Frank Darabont

The script is the director's bible. Knowing this, directors kill for a good script. Without a worthwhile screenplay, one simply can't make a satisfying film. However, even with a tight script, there is no guarantee of success. Making film involves many phases and compromises that influence the final product. Films are actually written three times: once as a screenplay, again during principle photography and, finally, the director and editor re-shape and re-write the screenplay into a finished film.

A screenplay is a blueprint for the construction of a film. Film is a collaborative medium in which the cast and crew will work with the director to interpret the story into a visual expression. There is a well-known expression every director says to the writer: "show don't tell." Screenwriters write what the audience sees and hears. If a character is superstitious, show him refusing to walk under a ladder.

Screenwriter William Goldman is often quoted saying, "Screenplays are structure." It is the framework or blueprint for something else, much as a musical score or architectural drawings when implemented become a concert or building. Writers work with different designs just as actors come from a variety of schools of acting. The most common structures are three act, five act and 27 scenes.

Dating from Aristotle, the three-act structure has been the basic structure of most plays and screenplays. The work begins with a set-up of the dramatic situation, moves to a confrontation and ends with a resolution that culminates with a climax followed by a denouement.

In a two-hour film, the first and third acts typically are around 30 minutes in length, with the middle act lasting about an hour. Noted screenwriter Syd Field breaks the middle act into two parts, as he feels the middle act often becomes slow. In dramatic writing acts are often broken up into scenes.

The five-act structure is based on Elizabethan drama, which originated during the Roman period. The five acts consist of exposition, rising action, climax (or turning point), falling action and resolution. The exposition provides the background information for the viewer to be able to understand the story. This act ends with an inciting incident that sets the story in motion. The rising action introduces secondary conflicts or obstacles that thwart the progress of the protagonist. The climax arrives when the drama turns for the protagonist. At this juncture in a comedy things begin to go well for the main character while in a tragedy they begin to go downhill. The falling action usually embodies some final suspense resulting from the conflict between the protagonist and antagonist. Finally the resolution has the main character either better or worse off than when the story began.

The 27-scene system reflects the true nature of screenplay structure. While the drama may unfold in Aristotelian or Elizabethan fashion, the screenplay itself is usually comprised of approximately 27 scenes, each one building upon another. *Driving Miss Daisy*, for example, is a film of 25 scenes with no discernable acts. As films are shot in multiple locations and then edited scene-by-scene this structure aids the director in shaping each sequence as if it were a short complete film within a larger context.

Key ingredients in a great script are clear plot, interesting characters, conflicts, sharp dialogue, cinematic situations, clever twists, a strong beginning and a super ending, all subservient to the central theme.

Scene Analysis

How does each scene:
- Advance the story and expand our awareness of the characters and the conflict?
- Follow from the previous scene?
- Lead to the next scene (the importance of transitions)?
- Advance the arc of the character(s) — what do we know that we didn't before?
- Feel rhythmically?

- Change relationship between the characters?
- Give information to characters?
- Give information to the audience?
- Resolve the dramatic need of the main character?

Plot

A clear and compelling story begins with the question "What if?" What if an out-of-work actor dresses as a woman? (*Tootsie*). What if a Hollywood producer is asked by the president to "fake" a war to boost the polls? (*Wag the Dog*). What if a mutant virus causes an unstoppable epidemic in a small town? (*Outbreak*). What if a man believes strongly in the core of the American judicial system, that a man is innocent if there is reasonable doubt? (*Twelve Angry Men*). What if the washed-up actors from a cancelled sci-fi TV show are pressed into a real war in space by aliens who think of the TV broadcasts as documentaries? (*Galaxy Quest*).

Each plot has a dramatic arc, a progression that comes to an inevitable and satisfying conclusion. As Jean-Luc Godard said, every film must have a beginning, middle and end, though not necessarily in that order. According to Robert McKee, author of the book *Story: Substance, Structure, Style, and the Principles of Screenwriting*, the plot should take the audience to opposite emotional extremes. Moments of comedy in an action film break the tension. A youth picture might balance silly and mature behavior. A courtroom drama explores both justice and injustice.

Characters

In the end, a director imbues a body of work with themes and perspectives that make the work unique. Donald Ritchie in *The Films of Akira Kurosawa* states: "Once the story is decided upon, the writing begins. In the act of writing, the form of the picture evolves. In simplest terms, and shorn of all philosophy, his [Kurosawa's] pictures are about character revelation."

Characters, believable people, give life to a screenplay. Their desires and deeds, and the actions they take to fulfill their desires, are the foundation of the story. The main character is usually referred to as the protagonist. We follow the protagonist's journey and the obstacles the character must overcome to achieve his or her goal. Most scripts begin with the main character about to begin or perhaps in the middle of their journey. What occurs before the beginning of the journey is termed *backstory*. This history of the character can provide plot, dialogue and mysteries to be solved. A thorough knowledge of the character's habits, actions and idiosyncrasies aid the actor and director in discovering specific behavior as well as the character's inner life.

What is the mission of your main character? To win $1,000,000 (*Slumdog Millionaire*)? This desire or goal will drive the plot. The emotional highs and lows expressed by the character make up his or her character arc, while what the character does and says shapes the story.

Besides a protagonist a screenplay may be populated with myriad characters, including the antagonist, a confidant and a love interest.

Conflict

Conflict is opposition that motivates or shapes the action of the plot. This is the heart of drama. A character wants something, and people and things just keep getting in the way of that person achieving the goal. Look at all the hurdles placed before the main character in *Slumdog Millionaire*: a kept girlfriend, a jealous host, suspicious and brutal police, a gangster brother.

Just as you must give your screenplay a main conflict in order to make your story exciting, so too must you create a main obstacle that your protagonist (hero) will struggle to overcome. To create your obstacle, ask yourself, "What is your protagonist's goal?" In other words, "What is he trying to do, get, or achieve?" "Who is preventing the protagonist from obtaining this goal?" The person who stands in his way is the antagonist (villain). "What is the protagonist's main obstacle to achieving his goal?"

Dialogue

Hitchcock comments on the relationship between dialogue and the image: "To me, one of the cardinal sins for a script writer, when he runs into some difficulty, is to say, 'We can cover that by a line of dialogue.' Dialogue should simply be sound among other sounds, just something that comes out of the mouths of people whose eyes tell the story in visual terms."

The key to a character is often revealed in the subtext of the character's actions and dialogue. Communications studies indicate that when we address one another, half the message comes from body language, 30 percent from volume and only 10 percent from the words. Subtext is the unspoken thoughts and motives of the characters who people the drama. It is what they really think and believe. To chase a child around a room shouting, "I'm going to eat you up!" is a demonstration of love, not hunger. The child is giddy with glee, hardly fearful of becoming a meal.

Cinematic

Hitchcock, explaining how he integrates the story and the setting in *Rear Window*, stated, "Here we have a photographer who uses his camera equipment to pry into the backyard, and when he defends himself, he also uses his professional equipment, the flashbulbs. I make it a rule to exploit elements that are connected with a character or a location."

Film is a visual medium. Show, don't tell. One should be able to watch a film with the sound off and understand the story. An excellent exercise is to determine what one image captures the essence of a scene. Great screenwriting is creating stinging images that speak volumes about the story, the characters and the theme. Orson Welles' fingers grasping the sewer grate in *The Third Man*, Dustin Hoffman ripping off his wig in *Tootsie*, Myrna Loy's expression when Frederic March returns from World War II in *The Best Years of Our Lives*.

Twists

Red herrings, plot twists, dramatic reveals, surprises and shocks are the bread and butter of movies: Clark Cable's line from *Gone with the Wind*, "Frankly my dear, I don't give a damn"; when their luggage kisses we know the lovers will unite in *And Now My Love*; the alien bursting from John Hurt's chest in *Alien*; the shower scene in *Psycho* that ends with the reveal of the untouched cash turns the picture from a crime of greed to a crime of passion; she's a he in *The Crying Game*; Eva Marie Saint turns out to be a government spy in *North by Northwest*; nice-guy Orson Welles in *The Third Man* dilutes penicillin to turn a buck; Toshiro Mifune tricks the evil lords to give the signal to attack in *Sanjuro*; the boy gunslinger in *The Unforgiven* has bad eyesight and has never shot a man.

These moments are highlights of cinema. Often when looking back on a film it is a particular or specific image or sequence that lingers with the audience long after the viewing. These are visualized moments that reveal and/or elucidate the story. These thrilling moments work because our expectations have led us to expect one thing and the director delivers another. It is the unexpected.

Beginnings

Directors have options in starting a film. The opening, like the closing, should embody the spirit and central theme of the film. Since you have the option, make the opening bold, exciting, dynamic, cinematic, eye popping, or hypnotic. Orson Welles begins *Touch of Evil* with a virtuoso 10-minute unedited shot that begins with a bomb placed in a car truck and ends with its explosion. The main characters, the themes and the main story points are all introduced in that one shot.

Kubrick's *The Shining* starts with a long shot of the family driving up the mountain to the lodge, symbolizing their spiraling journey into isolation and madness. He starts his film *Dr. Strangelove* with the refueling of long-range bombers in mid-air, thus immediately enveloping the audience in a world of sex and violence juxtaposed with irony and absurdity.

The notion of starting the picture off with a bang also applies to the introduction of your main characters. Since you have the choice, introduce them in a unique manner. Reveal them, come upon them, have them step out of the shadows, truck into them quickly. An excellent example is the way Fritz Lang introduces Peter Lorre as the child murderer in *M*. The camera is motivated to pan from a little girl bouncing a ball off a large post to the post itself. On the post is a wanted poster for the child murderer. Suddenly a shadow falls over the poster, a profile of the killer, Peter Lorre. The shot is a portent of things to come (the girl is murdered shortly after this scene). It is symbolic of his character, a mere shadow of a man. It's graphic. It condenses story. It's ominous. And, it is original.

Endings

The screenwriter plays with the audience's expectations to build to a satisfactory climax. The ending consists of a climax and a denouement. The climax is the height of the story. The impact of the climax is proportional to the level of suspense. The word *climax* is derived from the ancient Greek meaning "ladder." The topmost step on the ladder is the climax. Coming back down the ladder is the denouement. The denouement is a series of events that follow the climax of a story, thus bringing it to conclusion.

While the climax is often exciting and even dangerous, the denouement is a reflection on what has just occurred. Sherlock Holmes fights and kills Moriarty (climax) and then reflects to Dr. Watson and Inspector Lestrade what makes a criminal mind tick (denouement). In *Psycho*, Hitchcock builds tension until the final reveal that Norman Bates has taken on the persona of his mother and, dressed like her, attacks and kills the private investigator. This shocking sequence is followed by a very lengthy, almost 10-minute denouement, during which the psychiatrist explains to the lovers how Norman's mind was twisted by a domineering mother. The final shot, or "tag," shows the car being winched out of the swamp. The audience knows the trunk contains the money stolen at the beginning of the film, reminding us again this was not a crime of greed, but of passion.

Some narratives conclude with an anticlimax. These wrap up the film with simple solutions to complicated stories. An effective anticlimactic ending can be satisfying, but one must be careful to make it work well and not seem like a cop out. *The War of the Worlds* builds to a climax in which we assume the world will end, only to find the hostile aliens succumbing to the common cold. If the aliens were to merely to run away at the end, the audience might feel cheated.

Conflicts are resolved that bring about a catharsis for the audience.

A film demonstrates real impact when the ending reverberates by concluding the central theme in a manner that speaks to the spirit of the story.

Here are several examples of effective endings that need no explanation if you have seen them. They sum up the story and surprise you with the universality of the moment:

Chinatown—"It's Chinatown, Jake."

Dr. Strangelove—Riding a nuclear bomb like a cowboy with the song "We'll Meet Again" playing over the mushroom clouds.

Greed—The dying man handcuffs himself to his killer, thus ensuring he won't escape the desert alive.

The Wizard of Oz—The first "It was all a dream" film with the people from Dorothy's life playing the allegorical characters in the film.

The Planet of the Apes—Rod Serling's trademark surprise ending with the Statue of Liberty buried in the sand.

The Graduate—He gets the girl, but the feeling captures the disenchantment with the '60s.

Bonnie and Clyde—A ballet of death in a hail of slo-mo bullets.

Godfather II—Michael sits alone in a cold, cold world.

It's a Wonderful Life—Clarence finally gets his wings!

8½—Life is a circus, isn't it?

The Central Theme

Sidney Lumet states, "When I first meet with the script writer, I never tell him anything, even if I feel there is a lot to be done. Instead I ask him the same questions I've asked myself: What is this story about?" All scenes are subject to the main theme. If a scene doesn't support this theme, it should be eliminated.

Sources for Screenplays

Directors (as all above-the-line players) are constantly on the look out for compelling material. To put all your efforts into only one piece would be a mistake. Timing, demand, desire and rights availability may not converge for years. Collect as many ideas, books and screenplays as possible. Be prepared with a variety of stories that, when made, create a body of work.

Directors constantly read scripts like a miner panning for gold. A completed screenplay is easily read in one sitting and can be placed on one of three stacks.

The first and largest pile contains rejected scripts. These are the stones in the riverbed. Poorly written, exploitative, derivative, stale, offensive, too expensive, uncommercial and esoteric are some of the reasons screenplays are discarded. There have been cases where golden nuggets are tossed aside in the rush to dispense with the avalanche of submitted scripts, but that's one of the risks directors take by plowing through so much material.

The second stack is fool's gold. These are screenplays that show some promise. Perhaps the director is interested in the writer's abilities, the setting or the potential of the story. From these scripts a writer may be hired to work on other projects, or a script could be marked for further development.

The third and smallest mound of scripts is gold. These are fully developed stories that, if given the green light, could rumble into production and possible glory. With the right director and cast, these scripts can be spun into solid films.

Choose screenplays with nonperishable topics. From the moment a director says, "This one's for me!" until opening night may take months or even years. Many television movies are made quickly because they want to capitalize on a compelling news story or recent event. But by the time a film is released, it may be too late to grab the public the way the event did when it was in the news. Always ask, "Will the audience be interested in this six to twelve months from now?"

A director can become known (pigeon holed) for working in a specific genre, such as horror, comedy or children's films. Hitchcock said he was a typed director, that if he made Cinderella, the audience would immediately be looking for a body in the coach. The director may feel trapped by success in a particular arena, but many escape this. Take, for example, John Ford and Akira Kurosawa, who made their reputations directing westerns and *jida** films, respectively. As their careers pro-

---

*Jidai or *jidai-geki* are Japanese period pictures.

gressed, they explored other genres. Stanley Kubrick was as comfortable with the horror film as he was with science fiction, war, romance and noir.

Ask if the subject matter is a good fit for your personality. One director might appreciate the opportunity to explore a story about capital punishment, while another would shy away. Personal taste is a factor. If a subject were distasteful to a director, it would be difficult to muster the level of interest and energy needed to realize a film.

The Academy of Motion Picture Arts and Sciences awards two Oscars every year for best screenplay. One for a script based on existing material, the other for an original screenplay. Both make entertaining and dynamic cinema. Original screenplays are unencumbered by the additional phase of adaptation. Completed screenplays based on other material bring their own set of challenges, such as reducing a lengthy and complicated novel to 90 minutes of visual storytelling.

Films made from existing material are usually based on stories from the literary world such as books, short stories, plays, magazine articles, newspapers, and historical events. Television shows, comic books and computer games also have cinematic potential.

Books

Books are a predominant source of material for movies. Agents, managers, studio executives and producers often have first-look deals with publishers, who let them see galleys (books about to be published). By getting first shot at them, insiders can bid on a book before it is released to the public.

The process is like a legal stock tip. There are so many books published that film companies and agencies employ teams of readers and book scouts to maintain pace with the flow of potential stories. Every studio, agency and production company has a story department solely responsible for finding, reading, analyzing and recommending material.

Where Do Scripts Come From?

- Ideas
- Images
- Characters
- Concepts
- Historical events

- Places
- Adaptations from short stories
- Dreams
- Memories
- Real events
- Fantasies
- Social issues
- Real-life experiences
- Magazine articles
- News stories

Bestselling books make potentially successful films in part because they have a built-in audience with their readership. Examples would include the *Harry Potter* series, and the works of Stephen King, John Grisham and Michael Crichton. It's no guarantee, of course, that a bestseller will make a great film.

It can take years for a book to make its way to the screen. Ken Kesey's *One Flew Over the Cuckoo's Nest* and J.R.R. Tolkien's *The Hobbit* are two examples of books that required time to mature in the public mind before the studios recognized their potential. Both these projects had dedicated producers and directors whose passion for the work moved it forward inch by inch, year by year, onto the screen.

Then there are the classics. *Ben Hur, Pride and Prejudice, Dr. Jekyll and Mr. Hyde, The Count of Monte Cristo,* and *The Time Machine* all received the Hollywood treatment, sometimes many times over. These are such compelling stories that a new generation of actors and moviegoers rediscover them. It is also possible to extract the story elements and modernize them to avoid any taint or expense associated with a "costume" drama. This has been done successfully with books such as Jane Austin's *Emma,* starring Gwyneth Paltrow.

The inherent challenge in adapting books is their length. Books are much longer than the average 120 pages of a screenplay. While both share key elements such as plot and character, book literature is often interior and contemplative, as opposed to films, which are visual and visceral. Novels are difficult to adapt because so much has to be either eliminated or telescoped to provide the experience we have come to expect from a movie.

Although popular books provide a built-in audience, even the most talented directors will have difficulty remaining true to the book while satisfying the moviegoing audience. Ang Lee's *Sense and Sensibility*, Nicholas Roeg's *Witches*, John Huston's *Moby Dick*, Erle Kenton's *Island of Lost Souls* and Rouben Mamoulian's *Dr. Jekyll and Mr. Hyde* made successful transitions. These films capture the essence of the narrative while at the same time managing to become true cinematic experiences. Stillborn results include Hiroshi Inagaki's *Samurai Trilogy*, Hector Babenco's *At Play in the Field of the Lords*, and Akira Kurosawa's *The Idiot*. These three films attempted to be so true to the complexities of the novels that they failed to properly translate into successful films.

Robert Mulligan's screen adaptation of Harper Lee's classic novel *To Kill a Mockingbird* is a superb film, and it succeeds in no small way due to the employment of voice-over. Voice-over is the omniscient sounding words or inner thoughts of a character in the film. Like a diary entry, it contains elements of intimacy and privacy, clueing the audience in to a world beyond the visual experience of what is on the screen. Voice-over is a useful tool in book adaptations to clarify the story of a complex novel squeezed into a two-hour movie. It is employed to good effect in Billy Wilder's *Sunset Boulevard* as well.

Directors make a choice when adapting a book: adopt it intact or capture only those portions which they deem the essence or through-line of the book. Eliminating certain plot points, characters, events or locations of the novel may upset those enamored with the book, but these decisions may make for a more coherent movie. Novels and screenplays are two different genres employing two different sets of rules for telling a story.

James Whale, when adapting Mary Shelley's oft-filmed *Frankenstein*, made the leap from "man versus nature" story to "monster" film. Though they share the same title, one would be hard pressed to see the similarity between the two stories, save for the basic premise. Ridley Scott's exciting and lean version of Philip K. Dick's *Do Androids Dream of Electric Sheep?* became *Blade Runner*. The film is a fully developed realization of one of three story lines Dick presents in the novel. I believe both Whale and Scott made intelligent choices adapting these two great novels. Whale chose to focus on the man-made-monster story, Scott, to jettison two of three major story lines in the book and focus solely on the replicants.

The great British stage and screen director Peter Brook made a faithful translation of a book in his screen version of William Fielding's *Lord of the Flies*. Upon reading the book and then screening the film, the two seem to be one and the same. And one of the reasons is that the book is not a novel but a 120-page novella, the same length as a screenplay. There was just the right amount of story and character development to make a rich and satisfying two-hour movie.

Short Stories

Lengthy or meaty short stories simulate the compact quality of the novella. The story can provide the necessary plot elements, and directors can fill in the rest with a vision they have about the setting and theme. This is what Spielberg did recently with Philip K. Dick's short story *Minority Report*. Similarly, John Ford expanded the short story *Stage to Lordsberg* into the classic western *Stagecoach*. These are both examples of interesting short stories that form the spine of the film narrative but also afford the director the opportunity to visually embellish the world of the story, adding complementary characters, situations and themes.

Plays

Plays are rich and suitable sources for adaptation to film. Many have made the leap from stage to screen, some more successfully than others. Plays are dialogue driven and set bound so filmmakers are challenged to find ways to "open up" a play and stage scenes in exterior settings.* Examples of splendid entertainment based on successful plays include William Shakespeare's *Henry V* (both the Olivier and Branagh versions), David Mamet's *Oleanna*, Michael Frayn's *Noises Off* and Reginald Rose's *Twelve Angry Men*. Sidney Lumet's cinematic directorial "take" shooting *Twelve Angry Men* was to shoot the first third of the film from a high angle to make the men seem part of a common event; the second shot from a normal or "eye level" position, as this part of the story was man-to-man debate; and the final third shot from a lower angle to

---

*Then there are the mavericks like Alfred Hitchcock who rise to the challenge of shooting a play by experimenting. His film version of the play *Rope* was shot in one long single take. Or take the example of his film *Lifeboat*, which although not a play, was shot on one single location, theatrically set bound on a lifeboat with only a handful of characters.

accent the claustrophobic feeling during the final deliberations of the defendant's fate having the ceiling loom over the characters' heads.

Theater depends on the audience suspending reality and entering a world of words, analogy and psychology. In film, however, the image is of a more visceral nature, one rooted in the illusion of reality. Plays are live, while the film experience is fixed. The cinema screening at 2 P.M. will be exactly the same as the one at 8 P.M. five weeks later. This immutable quality injects some distance between the viewer and the screen.

Magazine Articles

Magazine articles have long been a popular source of film material. Ever since Charles Dickens, Mark Twain and Jack London were serialized in weekly magazines, audiences equated the freshness of a new publication with recent and timely literature. Short stories, exposés and in-depth journalism make magazines a target of scrutiny by producers, directors and agents. *City by the Sea*, based on an Esquire article by Mike McAlary, is an example of a recently made De Niro vehicle film transposed from magazine article to the screen. Other successful translations include *Urban Cowboy, Goodfellas*, and *Saturday Night Fever*.

News Headlines

A tradition exists of producers and directors pouncing on a news item or grabbing front-page headlines and turning them into a film. Often sensationalistic, these stories play on the fascination we share about what really went on behind the scenes. Films such as *The China Syndrome* (a near nuclear plant meltdown) by James Bridges, Menahem Golan's *Delta Force* (dramatizing the Israeli raid on Entebbe) and Barbet Schroeder's *Reversal of Fortune* (exploring the Sonny Von Bulow trial) brought current events to the big screen.

History

Historical events provide a bottomless quarry of source material. Truth is often more compelling than fiction. From Lon Chaney to

Schindler, Roman gladiators to World War II code breakers, FDR to JFK, history provides filmmakers with ample dramatic material with which to shine light on the human condition. History also has the benefit of being a voluminous source of chronicles in the public domain.

Television

Besides literary sources, film has also capitalized on that other great American cultural phenomenon, television. From series, to cartoons, TV movies and even game shows, a popular show on television, in part because of its familiarity, has potential to be a crowd-pleasing film as well. The grosses on *Scooby Doo, Star Trek, Twilight Zone, Charlie's Angels, The Powerpuff Girls* and *The Avengers* attest to the ease with which a television show can vault to the big screen. And the opposite is true as well. Television looks to the popularity of a film and then develops a series, such as MGM's hit 1998 film *Ronin*. Of course, for every success story there are many more failures. *The Flintstones, Lost in Space* and *Rocky and Bullwinkle* all tanked as feature films.

Foreign Films

Hollywood producers are fond of purchasing the rights to an interesting foreign language film and "Americanizing" it for local consumption. Producers screen the original film and determine its potential for an American audience (the guesswork involved in the decision to make a film from a screenplay is reduced considerably when the script has been realized successfully in another format). These are films that are often big hits in their own country, but because of language and/or social idiom, never reach our shores. Or, if they do, they are shown in small art houses only. Examples of films in this vein include the French film *Three Men and a Baby*, the Dutch film *The Vanishing*, and *The Magnificent Seven*, based on the Japanese classic *The Seven Samurai*.

Comic Books

Films begin their visual life in production as storyboards, which bear a remarkable similarity to the comic book format. So it is an easy jump to adapt a story in the frame-by-frame format of a comic book to that of the shot-by-shot format of a movie. In William Savage's book *Commies, Cowboys, and Jungle Queens: Comic Books and America, 1945–1954*, he informs us, "Comic books crystallize the social and political problems of a troubled period in American culture. In addition to their entertainment value, comic books offered a unique world-view to a large segment of the American public in the confusing decade following World War II. Millions were distributed to service personnel during the war years, and by 1945, adults as well as children were reading an astounding 60 million comic books per month. These books treated such contemporary concerns as the atomic and hydrogen bombs, growth of international Communism, and the Korean War, and they offered heroes and heroines to deal with such problems."

Comic books are a fascinating blend of literature and art. There has been a remarkable increase in the leap from printed matter to screen in comic book characters of late. Realizing such dynamic fantasy characters on screen has hit a chord with American audiences. The heroes of many of these comics, such as *Batman, Superman, The Hulk* and *Daredevil*, embody values such as truth, justice and the American way boiled down to simple homilies.

Computer Games

Computers have provided a wealth of new material, particularly in the arena of computer games. The youth market was raised on computer games. *Lara Croft: Tomb Raider, Super Mario Brothers* and *Final Fantasy* are only a sampling of characters that have made the jump from Game Boy to silver screen.

The Pitch

The purest form of development, one that is employed by the studios, is the purchase of a pitch. A writer and/or director meet with an executive and pitch a story. If the executives feel strongly that the idea would make a terrific film, they enter into a step deal in which the studio or producer pays the author(s) to put the story down on paper. By entering into this type of deal the author has sold the story rights to the developers. It is easier to pitch a story and be paid to write it down than sell a screenplay after it has been written. Screenplays take a long time to write and there is little guarantee it will ever generate income (writing a screenplay on speculation, with the hope of selling it as a finished product, is called a "spec" script). If a buyer shows interest, an author can negotiate a larger fee for a spec script than for a step deal. As the saying goes in Hollywood, ideas are cheap, but great screenplays are hard to find.

Pitching is an art. It begins with a solid story worked out in detail and employs all the elements of drama: timing, clarity of speech, physical gestures, props, pace, energy, command and performance. It is the goal of the writer or director pitching an idea to leave the pitch meeting on a high note, with the executive who has just heard the pitch wondering, "How can I live with myself if I don't grab this project and develop it for our company?"

The pitch is akin to a treatment. It maps out the essence of the story, describes the main characters and their dilemmas, and gives a smattering of dialogue and detail. It should be short and sweet. The presentation should be clear and energetic. Al Pacino's first starring roll was in *Panic in Needle Park*, allegedly pitched and sold on the one liner "Romeo and Juliet on junk."

One of the pitfalls of pitching is that it is easy for an executive or producer to say "no." If fact, they might interrupt as you begin the pitch with a pass on the project, stating, "We have something like that in development now. What else have you got?" One can study three terrific spoofs on pitching in the opening shot of Robert Altman's insider film *The Player*.

Securing Rights

Investigate the availability of a story before planning to make it. Producers and studios often hold onto the rights of stories and scripts as a commodity. Sometimes rights are already promised to a producer or production company that has a deal with a particular studio. Only if the rights are unencumbered can you begin the process of negotiation.

Consider the cost. The fee for the rights may be prohibitive. It is a seller's market, so the purchase price and the price of the option, although negotiable, are set by the owner. In the fast and furious world of movies, the amount of money spent on material ranges from one to millions of dollars. Since everything turns on the quality of the screenplay, vying to secure the rights to a good story is worth all the orchestration.

An entertainment lawyer conducts a title search to determine the status of the desired material. Once the owner has been identified, you are in a position to negotiate a fee for the rights. Rights can be granted in perpetuity (an outright sale) or for a limited time (an option). Purchasing the material outright gives one the right to make (or not make) the film as well as to alter the material. An option gives one the right to create a screenplay, secure the financing and put the story into production before the option expires. Once the option expires the rights revert to the original owner.

Options are traditionally granted for one year with an option to renew for an additional six months to a year. The seller can option the material to the buyer year after year if they so choose, as long as no other interested party makes a better offer.

To venture into a film without having secured story rights is one of several taboos in the business. At some point in the process the author will want to be paid. The farther along one is with an unprotected project, the weaker the negotiating position for the buyer. There are cases where a director will spend the time and money to develop a screenplay in order to demonstrate to the original author that his or her "take" on the movie approach is valid and dynamic, thus winning the approval of the author and eventually securing the rights. But this is a risk.

Every studio has a team of lawyers in its Business Affairs office to ensure that their ownership policies are clear and effective. This office finalizes all deals with writers and directors, and it is the directive of the business affairs officers to protect the studio. Individuals claiming they once pitched the director a similar story and they should now be compensated have slapped many hit films with nuisance suits. Luis Buñuel once worked for Robert Florey, who was making *The Beast with Five Fingers*, starring Peter Lorre. "At his suggestion," said Buñuel, "I thought up a scene that shows the beast, the living hand, moving through a library. Lorre and Florey liked it, but the producer absolutely refused to use it. When I saw the film later in Mexico, there was my scene in all its original purity. I was on the verge of suing them when someone warned me that Warner Bros. had sixty-four lawyers in New York alone. Needless to say, I dropped the whole idea."

A screenplay, book, play, short story, game, comic book, television show or film is bought or optioned and then developed into a workable screenplay. The development phase can be skipped only if the material purchased is a polished screenplay ready for production. The development process involves the contracting of a writer (or writers) to work with a director or story executive to develop the material into a screenplay. The writer(s) is almost always hired on a "step deal." In this contract, the buyer agrees to pay the author a certain sum of money at each step of the writing process. These steps include treatment, outline, first draft, second draft and a polish. If the film is produced, a bonus fee is paid to the writer on first day of principle photography. Should the film perform so well it generates profits, and if net points have been negotiated, after the studio recoups its negative cost, the writer(s) receives additional compensation. At any step the author's services can be terminated.

Producers seem to feel that only so much can be squeezed out of writers, and that when the creative process slows down it is necessary to replace them. As a result, the Writers Guild of America has established a board of review whereby other writers determine, once the film has been completed, who wrote what on which draft and award credits accordingly. The creative process is quixotic at best so sticking with one author may reap the same results as hiring a team of writers. Many wonderful ideas have been spoiled and diluted by tampering and rewriting. On the other hand, another saying in Hollywood goes, "Great screenplays aren't written, they're re-written." Screenplays often go through many drafts, so a director is looking for not only the right screenplay, but also the most suitable draft of that screenplay.

If a project dies or languishes in "development hell," it does so at the bidding of the studio that has spent the money to buy the rights and hired writers to develop the screenplay. The studio has a tidy sum of money tied up in each project they develop, and each studio develops hundreds of scripts a year. At a certain point stipulated in the writer's contract, the original author has the right to try and sell the project elsewhere if the studio decides to stop pursuing the project. This is a turnaround clause commonly valid for one year, after which the rights revert once again to the studio.

If the author and his or her representatives manage to set the project up at another studio or independently, the studio will demand all fees and interest on the money be paid back in order for the rights to be transferred. Even if the author is unsuccessful in taking advantage of the turnaround, the studio can be approached at any time after the turnaround and made an offer on the material, as any development company prefers its money be returned on a dormant project.

The rights to a story are almost always obtained through an entertainment lawyer. Exceptions are stories in the public domain and screenplays written directly for the screen by the director. Public domain refers to the status of publications that are not protected under copyright. In most cases this can be calculated as 50 years after the death of the author. The copyright laws have been adjusted several times, and some rights have reverted to the author's estate, thus prolonging the copyright. Work created before 1900 is more than likely to be in the public domain. A lawyer should check the copyright on work in the 20th century.

A director is at risk with public domain material. If one subscribes to Carl Jung's theory that there preexists a collective unconscious, nowhere is it more evident than in Hollywood. At any moment an executive in Century City can have an inspiration: "Hey! Lets make a movie about Hannibal!" On the same day another executive across town in Burbank is responding to a pitch from a young author who sells him the idea, "Hannibal! Not the guy in the mask, but the one with the elephants!" Before you know it, three studios are making a *Hannibal* movie. And how about those Crusades? And isn't Alexander Great?

An example of the phenomenon of an idea being seized on simultaneously by two or more unsuspecting producers was the competition between Dustin Hoffman and Robert Redford over their respective rampant virus pictures. The race was running neck and neck for months of well-publicized casting and preparation. Redford finally backed down when it became apparent his story, *The Hot Zone*, would be ready for market weeks after the Hoffman project, *Outbreak*.

The Bible, Chaucer's *Canterbury Tales*, all Shakespeare, Mark Twain, H.G. Wells and Dickens are free of copyright. The books and stories of Isaac Asimov, Anne Rice, Stephen King and Michael Crichton are all owned either by the author, the author's publisher, or the author's estate.

All literary material is registered with the United States Library of Congress. Screenplays are also registered with the Writers Guild of America. Any question as to who controls the rights of a literary work can be resolved by contacting the original publisher, noted on the inside jacket of the book or printed story.

Kurosawa stated that screenplays are made by talking. The author, whether working alone, with a partner or with a director, talks though each and every scene to make it part of a whole. They act out sequences, challenge each other and allow their imaginations to soar. They listen to music to get a feel for the emotional content, watch other movies, see plays, and go to the circus. Lumet advises, "Thrash things out in advance. We are two different people trying to combine our talents, so its crucial we agree on the intention of the screenplay." Luis Buñuel would meet with his writer every afternoon and over a martini he would ask the writer to tell him a story, not the one upon which they were currently working, just a story.

Find a writer who understands screen writing or screen adaptation. Write it yourself if you have to. Find ideas in the everyday: television, books, newspapers, and so forth. Then hold on to that script for dear life because it will be your best route to the director's chair.

The French coined the phrase *auteur* in the late 1940s, affording the film director the status of creator. While it is true that directors create a film by nimbly combining literature, design, music and theater, they couldn't do it without their team of artists: the screen writer, cinematographer, set designer, editor, composer and performers. Only if the director is also the screenwriter* can one really consider the director the author

---

*One of the most interesting debates in the film industry is the granting of a possessory credit. Credits are important to all the key players in a film, as they would be in any performance work. The director comes closest to an author in terms of credit by having his or her name placed in what is referred to in contracts as "final position." This is the most prestigious position in a film's credit listing. As soon as the director's name disappears, the film "begins." In the early days of cinema, often the producer claimed this choice position in the lineup of credits. As the one providing the capital to realize the film, the producer was not challenged until 1934, when George Cukor won the right to place his name in this ideal position. It was at this point in film history that it became acknowledged that directors were primarily responsible for the creative melding of the elements that make up a film. It was he or she that created an environment where a true gestalt might occur, in which the whole was greater than the sum of its parts. It rarely happens, and when it does, the director can surely be credited as the one chiefly responsible. A possessory credit is one in which not only does a director receive the final credit (both on the screen and in all paid advertising) but also an initial or presentational credit, as in "A Woody Allen Film," or "Miramax presents a Brett Ratner Film," etc.

of a film. Whereas a writer writes a book, poem, play, short story or film script in private, a team of crafts people and artists makes films.

In the end, regardless of how many people contribute to the film's making, the glory — and the responsibility — ultimately lies with the director. A director may have a dream, witness an event, have a single image or hear a song, strike a chord, which when developed, becomes a fabulous screenplay. François Truffaut once had a vision of a car sliding down a steep snow-laden road. From this one image he conceived *Shoot the Piano Player*. Film material sources are limitless.

◄◄ **2** ►►

Cast

Always get more sleep than your actors.
— Orson Welles

Actors are the life's blood of any show. The best screenplay is only as good as the players performing the text. If the screenwriter is the heart, the director the brain, the cinematographer the eyes, the mixer the ears, then the actor is the blood that pumps life into the undertaking. Or to use a construction analogy from actor Sean Penn, "The difference between being a director and being an actor is the difference between being the carpenter banging the nails into the wood, and being the piece of wood the nails are being banged into."

From initial casting sessions, to read-throughs and rehearsals, through wardrobe and make-up checks, shooting, looping and public-ity, the director and actor share a special bond. They establish a mutual confidence wherein directors can encourage actors to stretch while actors feel comfortable asking for the space to experiment.

Except in unique cases, a director employs actors to people the story. These actors breathe life into the words and characters *suggested* by the screenplay (suggested because the script often serves only as a rough guide-line, which goes through an alchemical transformation from paper to film). This change begins with the actors. It is through actors that the director maintains the emotion of the picture. As noted film director Alfred Hitch-cock said, "Our primary function [as directors] is to create an emotion and our second job is to sustain that emotion." With such a crucial task rest-ing on the director's shoulders, it behooves him or her to understand the temperament and mindset of the actors selected to play parts in the show.

There is a direct relationship between the harmony on set and the precision of a professional cast. When the performances are convincing, the set hums. When they aren't, tension and delays build up. This is why directors are fond of assembling an acting ensemble with which they can collaborate, picture after picture. This repertory approach is desirable because the director and cast, who have an established rapport, can quickly re-establish it upon beginning a new project. Actors intuit the direction; directors sense where the performance is headed. The director and actor cultivate a shorthand to communicate, and, because it is almost instantaneous, the company moves all the faster. Examples of effective pairings include Scorsese and De Niro, Mamet and Pidgeon, Spielberg and Dreyfuss, Ford and Wayne, Hitchcock and Kelly, Coen and McDormand, Kurosawa and Mifune.

Casting

Casting is 50 percent of the director's work. Hiring the best available actors makes for a smooth and rewarding shooting process. If the director then creates an atmosphere conducive to deep emotional work or one relaxed enough to free up those actors' best instincts, the performers will feel valued and thus eager to explore the role further.

Casting is the process by which one determines the actors available and willing to play a part in the film. The efforts of the entire production office are involved in this crucial process. Casting directors organize and oversee the entire proceedings, often supervising preliminary auditions to whittle down the field in order to present a select group to the director. The production manager arranges a space to audition and contacts agents for submissions. The director selects the actors. Finally, the producer negotiates the contracts.

Actors, like directors, seek out good material. The best way to entice an actor to a role is to have a great screenplay.

I will work with a director who has good material because at the end of the day, that's what counts.

— Javier Bardem

There are two methods of cast selection: the audition and casting a known actor. In either case, factors to consider, aside from talent and suitability, include availability (dates may not jibe with the production schedule), affordability (the budget may not allow for their quote — see glossary) and credit (some casting decisions can be solidified only after successful credit negotiations).

The audition is a brief period (on average 10 to 15 minutes) wherein actors demonstrate their skill. They may read from the screenplay, perform a prepared scene, and/or improvise a situation indicated by the script. During this time, the director gauges not only the actors' abilities, but also their demeanor, persona, voice and physicality.

To find the best actors for the parts, it is important to cast a wide net and keep an open mind. A director might see hundreds of actors before making a selection.

To locate these performers a casting director will use every avenue available, including submitting a character list to breakdown services,* contacting agents and managers, advertising at acting schools in local papers or trade publications.

The character breakdown is written specifically to weed out absurd cast choices, yet is general enough to allow for the quirky surprise. Describing the character of Sally as a "woman in her thirties" is too broad and might encourage a thousand actresses to audition (including those who are 18 and "play older" or those who are 40 and insist they are still an "ingénue"). Conversely, to say Sally is "a slight woman in her thirties, fragile like Laura in *Glass Menagerie*, with blond hair, brown eyes, has a lisp in a South African dialect, and six fingers on her left hand" is too rigid a description and may reap no hopefuls. A compromise in the character description would encourage a moderate number of actresses who might fill the part. Consider that hair color can be changed, eye color may not be important, accents can be learned and body parts can be altered with special prosthetic make-up. Only a role calling for a

*Breakdown Services, Ltd., is the communications network and casting system that provides integrated tools for casting directors and talent representatives. With offices in Los Angeles, New York and Vancouver, Breakdown Services maintains affiliate relationships with sister companies in Toronto and London. Breakdowns are complete synopses of the characters contained within scripts. Talent representatives then download from the Breakdown Services website 50 to 60 pages of casting information. They use the resulting breakdowns to understand what roles are available and then submit their actors and actresses for these roles.

specific special trait or unique talent requires more precise descriptions, such as when casting an extremely obese man, a little person, or a professional sword swallower.

The production company collects head-shots (photos and resumes of actors) from agents or through the mail. From these photos a group of actors to audition for the casting director and/or the director is selected. Actors are seen at ten- or fifteen-minute intervals during the auditions. The actor enters a room and meets the director and casting director. After brief pleasantries, the actor reads from the screenplay or recites a prepared monologue.

The director may require the actor to read the text again, asking for an alternate interpretation. A brief improvisation may be requested. The director and casting director thank the actor, make notes and the next actor is called in.

The director and casting director may not be the only ones present at the audition. The producer might choose to observe the proceedings, another actor or assistant may be called upon to read opposite the actor auditioning, or a camera person might be employed to videotape the audition. Fewer personnel are better, so the actors can demonstrate their skills with few distractions. Of course the case can be made that an actor who cannot perform in a room full of observers might freeze up on a crowded set.

Sometimes referred to as a cattle call due to large turnouts, an open call is an opportunity for actors to try out for the parts listed. Although time-consuming, an open call can reap interesting choices for roles. They are particularly effective when a company is shooting in a distant location and seeks local talent for small speaking parts, silent bits and extras. Those who attend an open call signal to the production company that they are eager to participate in the movie.

There are three considerations in evaluating the audition: the particulars of the character, the juxtaposing of this actor with the other cast members, and the gut response of the director. These ephemeral qualities are often referred to as chemistry. Matching one actor with another may result in emotional sparks, friction or total lack of response.

At a callback an actor is asked to audition once again. This affords the director an opportunity to come to a decision about a performer. At this time the director may ask two actors to perform opposite one another to ascertain their chemistry.

Stars and established actors often do not audition. The costs associated with filmmaking are so great it may be mandatory that a known actor be "packaged" with a script and director. This high-priced talent is a security measure guaranteeing the finished product will gain attention. One can visualize a known actor in a role based on the knowledge of their previous work.

The director and producer will finalize casting once all potential candidates are explored. The director needs a keen eye and ear to evaluate both the actor's talent and their suitability for the part. Take your time. Casting too quickly means a better actor might be ignored.

While it is important to cast as wide a net as possible to find the lead actor, bear in mind the antagonist should be given as much attention as the hero or heroine. The drama is only as good as the obstacles facing the hero. If the villain of the piece is a compelling character played by a dynamic actor, it makes for high drama. In the first two *Spiderman* films, Peter Parker was pitted against the Green Goblin and then Doctor Octopus. The second film is the more compelling in part because the villain is more of a threat. Films such as *Dr. Jekyll and Mr. Hyde, Silence of the Lambs, Cape Fear, Shane, Sanjuro* and *The Adventures of Sherlock Holmes* are elevated by the antagonist. Boris Karloff, with no dialogue, made *Frankenstein* a classic.

An actor's availability is an important factor when considering the production schedule. Actors sign a contract with an "on or about" target start date. The production can be delayed by a few days without jeopardizing the casting. A delay of a few days is not uncommon, a fact recognized by the Screen Actor's Guild. However, if a major postponement moves the first day of principle photography to more than a few days off the target date, casting can be jeopardized. An actor may at such time opt to take on other employment. Casting may also be affected if a lead actor negotiates a stop date (see glossary).

Ten Basic Steps to Casting

1. Create character descriptions for all speaking roles including physical type, age and personality.
2. Solicit submissions (pictures and résumés) from talent agencies through Breakdown Services or direct calls.
3. Sort through submissions and pull pictures that fit the characters.

4.   Pre-screen actors that might be right for the part but whose work you are not familiar with.

5.   Callback pre-screens and additional actors for a director's casting session.

6.   Discuss choices and make offers.

7.   Negotiate deal points with actors' agents.

8.   Create a deal memo for each hired actor.

9.   Have production contact actor with call time and cross your fingers.

10. Spend time with your actors prior to rehearsals.

Actors have to be attracted by a part. Matching or even surpassing their quote may not be enough incentive to play a part they consider uninteresting, poorly written or damaging to their career. More than anything actors want a challenging role. Fees and credits are important, but the part is everything.

One of the more delicate negotiations between producer and agent is the credit to be awarded the actor for their work. It's possible for a director to become involved in actor negotiations, especially if the director doesn't want to lose the actor over fee or credit. A wise producer negotiates credit "at the discretion of the producer," which frees the company from any binding credit issues. Most agents, however, want their clients to be guaranteed the most important credit they can wheedle out of the producer. Credits are an integral part of an actor's quote. If a role guarantees $10,000 a week and fourth billing, that will be the quote for the actor's next picture. This is the position from which the agents negotiate for their client. Therefore, if a producer has only $8,000 a week to offer, giving the actor better billing might offset the reduced fee.

Actor negotiations are a balancing act in which the agent strives to get the actor as much money as possible but not to blow the deal by insisting on too high a figure for the production company to meet. Agents receive 10 percent of the actor's salary so the more money the agent can negotiate, the higher their commission. That's not to say actors are not also interested in a healthy fee. Very few actors work 52 weeks in a year.

Some actors can be so excited about a role, flattered and eager to begin work, they might very well blurt out to the producer, "I don't care, pay me what you will," which is hardly a strong position from which to negotiate a deal. That's where the agent comes in. The agent has to weigh how much their client wants to play the part against how eager the production company (primarily the director) is to land the actor. Judging where that magic number lies makes negotiating an art.

Sometimes negotiations take a long time. Agents and producers play stalling games to see how the collaboration between the actor and director unfolds. If the director becomes more excited about the actor, the agent's position is fortified. If the director has other choices should this actor fall out or if the agent drives too hard a bargain, the producer's position grows stronger.

The catchall phrase in the film industry for contract or personality meltdown is "artistic differences." When there are differences of opinion causing contract negotiations to deteriorate (often over credit more than cash), one reads in the trade publications how "artistic differences" caused the parties to go their separate ways.

"Artistic differences" also imply a settlement of some kind for the actor's salary. If actors are fired from a production, they must be paid their full salary. The clause protecting the actor's salary is termed "pay or play." The production company must play them or pay them if during pre-production, or even in the first days of shooting, it becomes clear that the director and actor cannot get along, and they may mutually agree to part. Even though the contract has not been fulfilled, all or at least a portion of the actor's salary will be paid, depending on the circumstances.

Besides contractual problems "artistic differences" can also mean just that, differences of artistic opinion on how a script should be interpreted. As the director has the "vision" for the piece, those whose vision differs from the director are usually the ones to leave the show.

To avoid the cardinal sin of firing an actor during principal photography one must cast wisely. As casting is not a perfect process, it sometimes becomes necessary to replace an actor. Replacing talent is not so difficult at the beginning of the shoot, even if it means reshooting a day or two. If the actor is replaced in the middle or toward the end of a shoot, all the sequences with that actor will require expensive reshoots.

There are cases when a highly paid actor and the director have an irreconcilable difference of opinion. The producer may consider the value of replacing the director against losing the actor. If the actor has shot more than 25 percent of the film, there is little choice for the producers, as the cost of both replacing the actor and reshooting a quarter of the film would most likely be financially prohibitive, in which case the director may be replaced.

The production company is signatory with the Screen Actors Guild (SAG), which has provided most of the boilerplate contract agreements in the codified contract. The agent negotiates the fee and credit, but may negotiate additional perks, such as a driver, entourage, personal make-up artists, stills approval and/or per diem. The SAG contract stipulates minimum standards related to travel, accommodations (both first class), working hours, working conditions and breaks. All potential violations and their penalties are also laid out in very specific formulas, changing with the size of the budget and nature of the show (television and feature shows have different parameters). Rule violations include meal penalties, overtime, and violation of turnaround (see glossary).

Actors are responsible for showing up (the first rule of show business), memorizing their lines and blocking and being professional. The Screen Actor's Guild agreement has protections for the producer should actors become unreasonable or difficult, stipulating that actors who display unprofessional behavior are subject to fines.

Read-Throughs

Before actual rehearsals begin the cast comes together to read the screenplay aloud. Watching actors breathe life into the script is a particularly stimulating moment for the director. Reading the dialogue to one another, actors imbue each beat, scene and even the through-line with shape and meaning. Rhythms, plot progression, negative space and shooting plans crowd in on the director at this reading. Insights gained around rewriting and shooting can be discussed after the reading with the writer and director of photography.

In these early stages the director and actors develop a mutual trust and common vernacular. Conferences on research, back-story, props, wardrobe, make-up, motivation and emotional levels generate raw materials from which the actor and director will create the character, once shooting begins. Establishing a rapport is important, for this bond is tapped when the creative process is underway.

Rehearsals

Rehearsing is a process wherein actors, guided by a director, discover and set a scene. The scene is blocked or choreographed in an approximation of the space at the location. As the scene unfolds, the beats that define the pace of the scene become clear. Interaction with the other actors, becoming accustomed to furniture pieces and props, all add to the effect. The director encourages the actors to explore and experiment until the scene feels right. A director must encourage an actor to run the full breadth of a trial and error, through rehearsals, discussion, improvisation and performance, to realize an effective and concentrated character.

Each director has to ensure all actors perform in a manner consistent with fellow actors. Actors are trained in a variety of styles, including the Stanislavski method, Meisner technique, and free form improvisation, to name a few. Some actors build a character through emotional memory, some by sense memory, and others use make-up, props and wardrobe. Two important keys to character development are the text and the responses and feedback from the other players. A few actors receive no formal training; others may have been trained in related fields such as mime or stand-up comedy. The director is the funnel through which all the actors' performances are channeled. It is for the director to shape the scene so that it becomes a unified whole.

Respect the various acting styles and encourage the actors to play off one another. The style of one will begin to blend with the other, and soon the entire company will be a unit. Although some actors are more adept than others at improvisation, it is an excellent tool with which a director can achieve remarkable results. Sidney Lumet states, "I use improvisation as an acting technique, not as a source of dialogue. If the actor is having trouble finding the emotional truth of a scene, an improvisation can be invaluable." Martha Coolidge also uses improvisation: "I had done a lot of improvisation in my early movies. I wrote them and they were based on improvisation, so I found myself very free to work with the actor's ideas. That's been the basic idea in all my pictures. Work with the actors. Let them feel comfortable. Take the actor's input. I like intelligent actors who have lots of ideas and bring a lot to the table. It's easy to say no when something doesn't work. What's really hard is when nobody has any ideas."

Improvisation can be particularly effective when making a comedy. Comedy relies in part on timing. Encouraging actors to use this technique puts them in a position to be natural, to find the proper time to interject or react, and to be inventive while in character. Casting comedians in comedy allows a director to create a scene, stand back, light the fuse and call action. This technique is risky, for the fuse might fizzle, but the potential results make it worthwhile.

Many actors, as part of their preparation, invent an elaborate history of the character as it relates to the text. As a result, a bit of action might arise that speaks volumes about the way the character behaves. Perhaps an actor has proposed that the character stuttered as a child, and that now, when flustered, reverts to a stutter under pressure. Though not written in the screenplay, the actor may have deduced from the writing that it was caused when the character was shunned as a child. The director could begin to see how the stuttering is a metaphor for the character's stops and starts in life. Perhaps the director expands on the idea and integrates it into the shooting and the editing.

During the rehearsal period, the following takes place:
• The director gets to know the actor.
• The actors bond with each other.
• The director and the actor develop a mutual trust.
• A character research method is devised.
• Scenes are shaped, beats are discovered, and business is created.
• The director and actor evolve a shorthand for communicating on set.

Character, pace, space and screenplay gel during rehearsals. The results from rehearsals are carried onto the set, where the sequences are polished and then shot. It benefits the entire film if each scene is rehearsed thoroughly. There should be adequate rehearsals prior to the shoot and if necessary, on the day of the shoot as well. Often there is little or no time for extensive rehearsals once production starts. The director is constantly balancing the demands of the production schedule with the resolve to make the best film possible. If a scene needs work, better to clear the set and rehearse until it is ready to be shot.

Checks

When production nears the start date, the cinematographer shoots tests of the actors in their make-up and their wardrobe. Last-minute decisions are made concerning style and color of the production as it relates to the characters in consultation with the art director. Adjustments made during principal photography can be difficult and costly. These tests ensure few surprises in the dailies.

The checks act as dress rehearsals. On set, just prior to rolling cameras, the assistant director will call for a final dress rehearsal, in the actual space, with all the props, set dressing, lights, appropriate cues and marks in place.

Shooting

The production team is divided between the men and women behind the camera (the crew) and those in front of the lens (actors). The director shuttles between these two stations spending the majority of time behind the camera orchestrating the shot. When it comes time to record a take, the director shifts to front-row-center and becomes part of the show as its sole audience.

Much of the work of creating a character is done in pre-production. Through research, consultations with the director and an art director, read-throughs and tests, the actor should have a pretty good idea of what is demanded from the character he or she plays at any point in the screenplay (read shooting schedule). Therefore a director can hope to have an actor arrive on set fully prepared to execute a sequence in a timely manner.

The director, as the sole audience member (see Chapter 7: Command), is aware of the emotional build in a scene and as it relates to the entire piece. Based on discoveries made in rehearsal, combined with the communication between actor and director, the correct emotional level can be found and executed when it is called for.

> *The first work of the director is to set a mood so that the actor's work can take place, so that the actor can create. And in order to do that, you have to communicate, communicate with the actors. And direction is about communication on all levels.*
> — William Friedkin

Directors employ many methods to work with actors. Some speak at length about the moment, the back-story, the desired emotions. Others say very little, counting on good casting and the actor having done their homework. Much of how a moment is created on set involves the interaction between the actors in the scene. Instinctively they know how to bounce off one another to reveal the proper beats. Director Stephen Frears suggests directing by listening. It is relatively easy to identify conviction through speech.

The only artistic communication with actors on set is through the director or with other actors. The actors and the director carefully mold the creation of a moment, or a beat within a scene. A scene may be made up of many beats, and it is the blending of these beats that gives the scene shape and emotional impact. When the director (with the editor) strings all the beats together, the emotional arc of the picture will be revealed. This is what Hitchcock refers to as "sustaining the emotion."

Professional actors come to the set knowing their lines, character and blocking. Speaking lines and reacting to the other players requires an actor be "in the moment" for a performance to be engaging and true. Trying to stay concentrated, with dozens of people on the set, it is easy to understand why an actor can miss a mark or flub a line. This is why take 2 (and 3 and 9 and 50) were invented.

Many departments help actors define a character. Hair, make-up, wardrobe and props assist in the design of the accoutrements they will use. This design, the look of the character, is further developed in tandem with the cast, director, art director and cinematographer.

Whereas the crew functions 10 to 15 hours a day at a steady, sometimes frantic pace, actors fluctuate between rest and performance. The difference in the intensity between these two intervals can be extreme.

Crew (including the director) arrive early, stay late, and labor constantly (with a break for lunch). Actors arrive on set and, after they are made up and outfitted in their wardrobe, wait for their call to act. Once the call comes, they must immediately get up to speed and performance level. After the scene is shot, they are sent back to their trailers to rest and wait for the next time they have to perform.

It is important for a director to understand this rhythm distinction, as it is easy to fall into the habit of thinking of the cast as one of the gang, part of the team. Even though cast and crew share meals, schedule, call sheets, and a common allegiance with the production company, they differ in their creative rhythm. Although integral and certainly key players, the director respects the pulse of the cast as different from that of the crew. The cast comes and goes, whereas the crew never leaves. Thus there exists a set of rules and considerations specific to actors in order to afford them the ideal environment in which to create a character. These include observance of an actor's eye line, access to a green room, consulting on the show's progress, adequate rehearsals and conferences on publicity.

The director needs to be aware of possible disturbances in the actor's sight line. It may prove distracting to the actor if people standing behind the camera are in their eye line. On a big set, the director and assistant director need to be constantly vigilant and sensitive to the actor's need for concentration.

A green room or trailer is a place where the actor can rest. Considering the rhythm of an actor on set — performing, resting, performing, resting — it is imperative there be a quiet space to which actors can retire should they so choose. This safe zone is an ideal place for the director to spend time and visit with actors, to chat, consult or to run lines. Keep actors in the know. They should be informed of changes to the schedule, be consulted on the show's progress and warned of pending rehearsals and breaks. At the outset of a production the director makes a decision whether actors will be allowed to see the dailies or rushes of the project. Many actors enjoy (or insist) on the privilege of viewing the material from the previous day's shoot. The 20 minutes or so of printed film will ultimately be reduced to a few minutes of screen time. There is always the possibility of an actor unhappy with his or her performance becoming self-conscious.

I think the most insulting thing you can do to a director is to challenge when he or she is satisfied with your interpretation.
— Dustin Hoffman

Green Room and Other Special Areas

- Is the green room (a holding area for the actors) far enough away from the set?
- Are there toilet facilities for the cast and crew? Is there someplace they can go to relax?
- Is there a quiet area away from the set where you can leave food out all day for the company?
- On an exterior shoot, is there a place where the company can

retreat from the elements if necessary (preferably someplace inside, such as a coffee shop)?
• Can a dressing room be rigged for the actors?
• Where will the actors apply their makeup?
• Is there an area off the set to store equipment?

Publicity plays an important role in filmmaking. Actors agree to allow the company use of their likeness to publicize the movie. Consult with them prior to allowing the press or television crews on set. Offer actors access to the slides scheduled to be production stills.

The cast is made up of primary characters, secondary characters, day players, extras, children, stunt players and animals. Primary characters carry the drama. The audience identifies with them. The plot hinges on their actions or inaction. A director's energy puts forward the story via the main characters.

Secondary characters represent the supporting cast, who shed light on the lives of the primary characters. A well-etched secondary character enriches a film. They may have several scenes or only a few lines. These actors should be rehearsed with the main actors to explore and reveal every nuance available in the scene and their relationships.

Day players perform small roles usually part of one scene or location. The news vendor, bus conductor or landlady interacts briefly with a primary or secondary character. These moments can be rich and revealing. Most day players do not rehearse until the day of the shoot. The director will have had a discussion with the actor about the sequence in which they will play, but the interaction between the main actors on location is explored just prior to shooting. This is where a director's skills working with actors pays off. With little time and much pressure, the director engages the actors in a brief rehearsal. If the scene needs additional time to gel, the director will take it without losing any patience with the day player, who could become flustered under pressure.

Extras, also called background, people the frame so it's empty or devoid of people. A main character stands in Grand Central Station at 5 P.M. on a Friday afternoon. The station is empty of commuters. No extras. The shot can only mean the film is a science fiction piece and it is the end of the world. A thousand extras rushing about from ticket counter to information booth to train track to concession stand create the illusion that the character is in Grand Central Station at rush hour. The assistant director hires extras through an extras casting service. During pre-production meetings, when asked how many extras are required to fill the background of each scene, a director is wise to request more than necessary. On set it is easier to eliminate a crowded frame than to fill an empty one. Often anyone available, crew-members, producers, pedestrians, can be pressed into service to fill in a frame with background extras should the company have too few extras on hand.

Working with amateur actors is often exciting due to their raw and natural quality, but there are often headaches and delays caused by missed marks and botched lines when using nonprofessionals.

Children are a special consideration when casting a show. They can only work so many hours (see Chapter 4: Budget), and they require multiple breaks in addition to schooling. There is less difference between a professional and amateur child actor than between a professional and amateur adult actor. Children with natural talent should be given minimal direction so as not to overload them with instruction. A successful method is to plan on several takes, adding a subtle layer of direction after each take until the child actor finds a groove. Adult actors performing with a child in a scene are often the director's greatest ally, as they can, on camera, with direct eye contact, coax the proper emotion from the child.

Stunt players are employed to perform a physically demanding action, either a stand-alone stunt (such as a pedestrian running from the speeding car driven by the main actor) or to double for one of the characters in the story (such as the driver of the vehicle). The art department is engaged to assist in making the stunt double look as much like the actor as possible. The better the match, the closer the camera can be to the stunt. Some actors like to perform in action sequences. Jackie Chan and Steve McQueen are well known as performers who performed many of their own stunts. They gave the audience an extra thrill because they were a recognizable part of the action. Insurance companies do not approve of primary actors performing stunts. If they become injured (as has happened with Jackie Chan on numerous occasions) then production either slows down or comes to a stand still while the performer heals.

An additional stunt category is that of a body double, usually employed for nude scenes. Some actors refuse to disrobe for the camera. In this case, the director storyboards the sequence to include a body double for the shots requiring nudity. It is prudent to have a body double standing by even if the actor is willing to disrobe, since the actor may have a change of heart. According to the Screen Actor's Guild rules, actors, even if they have consented to go nude, are not obligated to do so.

Actors like to give 110 percent to their work. But even the most professional actor knows there are limits. Tricks with the camera can be very helpful in solving issues of actor limitations. Sean Connery said to Terry Gilliam when shooting a sequence in *Time Bandits*, "I'm not going to let you see me get on the horse because I won't look good. So what I'll do is just rise up in the stirrups and you can film me sitting down."

Tricks in editing can also be very helpful in solving issues of actor limitations. Actors who say "um" and "ahh" can be edited in such a way as to make their speech smoother, longer, slower, and faster, etc. A classic example of physical editing, culled from an accident, would be the scene in George Stevens' *Shane* when the good guy (Alan Ladd) faces off for the first time with the bad guy (Jack Palance). The scene takes place at a farmhouse with the rancher talking with the farmer about water rights violations. Each one going to the well, the two hired guns, Ladd and Palance, size each other up over a cup of water. As the scene comes to a climax, the Jack Palance character gets back on his horse in an eerie manner, that is, he seems to defy gravity as he slinks back into his saddle like one of the devil's minions. The creepy quality in the scene was discovered when the director took the shot of Palance getting off his horse, printed it backward, and used it for the shot of Palance getting back on the horse.

Animals bring their own set of challenges. The key to working with animals is to have them trained prior to shooting to do whatever is required in the script. Because humans cannot tell, many animal parts are played by multiple animal actors. For example, there were 30 pigs playing the lead roll in *Babe*. There was a pig to talk, a pig to open the gate latch, a pig to lie down, a pig to roll over, etc. Since the voice of Babe was consistent, it all looked to the audience like one pig. A pig in the audience, however, would have been very confused. Directors rely on the animal trainer to direct the animal in a scene. As with children, the actor playing in the scene with the animal can be helpful in terms of performance.

Looping

When the show is shot and edited, work on the soundtrack begins. Actors participate in that part of the soundtrack development called looping, or ADR (automatic dialogue replacement). It is a challenge for the sound mixer to record perfect location sound. Any number of disturbances can dirty a track, including airplanes, traffic, dog barks, etc.

If necessary, actors are called to a dubbing studio to re-record their dialogue while looking at themselves on a screen. The goal is to match the lip movement on the screen with the dialogue so the audience will not observe any mismatch. Actors may have to replace anywhere from a few lines to the bulk of their text.

Actors' contracts include several days of looping, as it is almost impossible for a director to get 100 percent clean production sound during shooting.

Publicity

Actors are encouraged to participate in the publicity campaign of a film in which they perform. Only their expenses are covered. The richness of the filming experience influences an actor's enthusiasm for the film and its subsequent promotion.

Actors are contracted for their "likeness," which includes stills from the movie that can in turn be used for publicity and/or advertising. The credit negotiation takes care of how and when and what size the actor's name can be employed in connection with the film. Often this area of advertising and credit are negotiated "as per industry standard," which, although a broad term, has been accepted as fair by both producers and agents. Producers aren't going to give star billing to a day player, nor would they neglect to give proper billing to the star.

Actors are involved in publicity and advertising on a purely voluntary basis. If they have enjoyed the experience and believe in the project, they will cooperate with the distributor to promote the film. Advertising makes the public aware of your film by purchasing advertising space, television and radio spots. Advertising is expensive. Publicity is free. An actor pleased with his or her experience on a worthwhile film is delighted to promote the project on a talk show, in the papers and at film festivals.

It's up to you, the director, to encourage every ounce of creativity from your actors. How you do it will vary from actor to actor, even from day to day. But your skill in choosing and dealing with the actors will in great measure determine the success of the movie. Choose them wisely, treat them with respect and trust, and you'll get what you paid for — maybe even more.

Ten Thoughts about Working with Actors

- Auditioning is hard.
- See your cast as your collaborators.
- Research is key.
- If you possibly can, rehearse before the shoot.
- Learn, and have respect for, how actors work.
- Don't forget to direct....
- ... but trust your cast, too.
- Actors aren't lab rats.
- Stunts are for stunt people.
- Sleep is the new black.

◀◀ **3** ▶▶

Crew

I am dependent on the talents and idiosyncrasies, the moods and egos, the politics and personalities, of more than a hundred different people.

— Sidney Lumet

With a good screenplay and an exciting cast, a director is well on the way to creating a dynamic film. The next step is to gather the team that will realize the project. A production calls for a professional and homogenous crew. Like casting, choosing a crew involves auditioning talented individuals considered a good fit for the production. And, like actors, availability and budget constraints may dictate selection.

Harmony during production is directly related to the precision with which a professional film crew works. Crews, for the most part, work steadily and efficiently for long hours. When the team works well, the set hums. In the same vein as assembling an acting ensemble, directors are fond of collaborating with the same production unit picture after picture. The director and crew have an established working relationship even before beginning a new project. Scorsese and Schoonmaker, Spielberg and Kaminski, Coppola and Tavoularis, Hitchcock and Herrmann are examples of sublime cooperation.

Movie crews can be relatively small or swell to over a hundred. The nature of the shoot, size of budget, whether it is an independent or a studio picture, dictate crew size. The director may engage with many or all crew members, but interaction is primarily between the department heads. These key crew members have, in turn, a team that effects the overall designs of the picture.

The key departments are production, casting, cinematography, art direction and sound recording. The department heads are the production manager, casting director, director of photography, art director, and sound mixer. In post, the director works with the editorial, sound and publicity departments, and the department heads are the editor, composer and publicist. All these department heads in turn hire their own teams.

The first consideration in selecting a crew is the location of the shoot. A film shot in Los Angeles, New York, Chicago, Toronto, Paris, London, Tel Aviv, Johannesburg, Bombay, Mexico City or Sidney is made all the easier because each of these locales has a thriving film industry. Major cities have access to ample professional crews. A director may choose to bring a director of photography and art director to the location, but even these key players may be found in a major metropolitan area. Elsewhere, it is necessary to transport key crew members, where department heads can usually fill out their ranks with local artisans.

As with any job application, crew applicants require a résumé. Just as the casting director weeds out head shots of actors, so too does a production manager or producer sift through crew résumés. It is standard procedure to call and check on the performance of a crew member from previous pictures, to learn how that individual might contribute to the planned production. Like the known actor who is not required to audition, a director can offer a job to an established key, such as a cinematographer, whose talent has already been demonstrated by a body of work.

To perform at peak capacity, a director must be confident that a department head will also give 100 percent. Directors do not interview all crew members. It would be wise, however, to reserve the right to veto the selection of a department head. If, for instance, the producer chooses a director of photography, the director should have the authority to reject the choice.

Consider availability when securing a team. Quality crews work exclusively on one film for several months. Toward the end of the production period crew members actively seek their next assignment. Except in Los Angeles, popular shooting periods are weather related. In New York good weather attracts more productions in the summer, spring and fall than during the winter. Therefore, Gotham-based crews may be spread thin in the warmer months and find themselves idle in winter. Union negotiations affect the availability of crews in a particular location. Six months before important negotiations with the Screen Actors

Guild, studios, concerned with potential union action, begin to stock-pile product. Scripts are rushed into production, and crews move from one production right into another. A strike in Canada would compel many productions to move back to the United States.

Production is a big, catchall category. Although run by a production manager, the company may have one or more producers associated with physical production. Titles during the production phase include *executive in charge of production, line producer, producer* and *associate producer.* The production department is responsible for disbursing the budget and managing the schedule. When directors require additional shooting time at a location, it is to the production department they turn.

Hired during pre-production by the producer, production managers oversee the day-to-day activities as well as look down the road to the last day of principal photography. They hire and negotiate deals for the bulk of the crew as well as organize vendors with whom the company can establish purchase orders. A production accountant manages the weekly payroll, and a payroll service is contracted to compensate the actors. The production manager files a daily production report, which is an account of the entire day's work: the time the crew actually arrived, when the director got off the first shot, insurance claims, and the exact time the assistant director called wrap. The call sheet is a prognosis and desired shooting plan for the day, whereas the production report indicates exactly what occurred and was actually accomplished.

The production manager's right hand in the production office is the production office coordinator (POC). This coordinator is the point person in a finely tuned unit. All telephone calls that come into the production office are filtered through the production office coordinator, who directs them to the appropriate department or crew member. Numerous calls come in during production. To handle the load accurately, directing the callers' requests requires effective phone skills. The production manager will have several assistants arranging locations, meals, transportation and product placement (see glossary).

The location manager and assistant director are vital members of the production team. The location manager finds and secures the locations for the film during pre-production and manages and massages them during production. The location manager is also responsible for moving the production unit from one location to the next and bedding them down for the night.

Location managers are the link between the production unit and the real world. Home and business owners often jump at the opportunity to rent their space to a movie company. The glamour, prestige and fee blind them to the reality of day-to-day film work. Once they witness firsthand how chaotic a movie set can be, and as they become concerned about the welfare of their property, the dazzle is lifted from their eyes and replaced by shock. The location manager must anticipate and placate this shift in the point of view of the property owner. It would be a reasonable expense to send the homeowners away on a two-week cruise to avoid all their concern and interference.

Shooting on location is fraught with conflicts regarding sound. When a barking dog or noisy neighbor disrupt a scene, the location manager has to take care of it. If a local airport needs to redirect its flight patterns, the location manager makes the call. Foot and car traffic immediately adjacent to the production unit, however, is controlled by the assistant directors.

If the location manager is the point person as the company makes it ways through the wilderness of movie making, the assistant director is the wagon master. The assistant director is responsible for adhering to the schedule indicated on the production board and the daily call sheet. Tactful and efficient, the assistant director is part cop, part drill sergeant and part Job.

The assistant director, through a system of second and third assistants, as well as production assistants, with the help of walkie-talkies,* orchestrates the minute-by-minute progression of the production. Keeping actors, lighting, grips, set dressing, and meals in a reasonable and efficient pattern is a challenge. With a mix of temperamental actors, long lighting setups, complicated camera moves and meal penalties, it is easy to imagine how assistant directing can be a test of one's abilities in a demanding if stimulating undertaking.

The assistant director has a team of at least three, which includes a second assistant director and a third assistant director. On days when the production company requires it, additional assistant directors are hired and strapped with walkie-talkies, when needed, for extras, traffic

---

*In the early days of Hollywood, there was no sound, so a director and/or assistant director shouted during a take. Before walkie-talkies, when sound came in, directors and assistant directors employed megaphones and hand and flag signals.

or crowd control. Special permits from local law enforcement agencies allow assistant directors or production assistants to stop pedestrian and automobile traffic from interfering with a shot. The first assistant director calls out "lock it up," meaning to stop the traffic, and then shouts for the shot sequence to begin. As soon as the director calls "cut," the assistant director informs the other assistant directors to "let 'em through," or release the traffic.

The production unit, or circus, as it is fondly called, is divided into three concentric circles. At the inner circle the camera resides and sequences are shot. The second outer ring houses the portable production support havens; make-up, hair, wardrobe, props, set dressing, grip and electric, camera truck, caterers, actor trailers and honey wagons. Bridging the inner and second circle is the second assistant's responsibility, primarily as it pertains to the actors. The second assistant director shepherds them between the inner and secondary circle. The third circle is everything that is not associated with the production.

As discussed in the previous chapter, actors follow a different schedule or rhythm than the crew. Actors rest or prepare between takes. Should they manage to find safe harbor from the chaos of the "circus," it is up to the second assistant director to locate and deliver them to set when needed by the first assistant director. So whereas the first assistant director controls the set or the inner circle, the domain of the second assistant director is the second circle. Whisking props, dressing, actors and refreshments onto the set falls under the purview of the second assistant director.

Because they are the crew members who spend time with the actors just prior to arriving on set, it is wise to consult the second assistant director, the make-up artist and the hair dresser. These three members of the team can be most effective in assisting the director by seeing to it that the actors arrive on set in a proper frame of mind. A catty hairdresser, a chatty make-up artist, or a second assistant director who tells an actor an off-color joke just before they arrive on set might disturb the actor's concentration. A second who is sensitive to the preparation that actors go through to perform well can be worth his or her weight in gold. Ferret out a good one.

The third assistant director is burdened with the copious amounts of paperwork associated with film production, including actor time sheets, call sheets and daily production reports. With this final addition to the team a first assistant director has enough help to control even the most difficult location.

The inner circle is the main set, the second circle the support vehicles, and outside these two rings, the real world. There are several members of the production team who travel from the production company to the production office, in and out of these three rings. Peripheral crew members include the production office coordinator, the publicist and the producer.

The production office coordinator remains the point person in the production office but ventures from the telephone to visit the set during production. Production assistants and/or drivers from the transportation department assigned to office duty normally handle the flow of paperwork from office to set. The production office coordinator can take advantage of lulls in the office to participate in the excitement of the main unit. These visits enhance the communication skills required in the production office to maintain efficiency.

The casting director usually completes his work during pre-production. However, casting can continue during production. Whether it's a case of an actor dropping out of a production or a day player hired on the day of the shoot, a good casting director can make immediate and significant artistic contributions to a film.

What does one look for in a key crew member? Is it collaboration? (Collaborating, or what Lumet refers to as the "shared experience," is addressed in Chapter 7.) Someone who will blindly obey orders? Some directors are most interested in working with a crew that will affect their ideas. Consider the dynamic between director and director of photography. If a director doesn't allow crew members, such as the cinematographer, to share their artistry, creative differences might arise. Conversely, a director hungry for input would be frustrated if the director of photography had no opinions or significant artistic contributions.

Do you want a cinematographer or a shooter? An editor or a cutter? Artist or journeyman? Some shows call for one over the other. A clever director can share a vision with a fellow artist. He may also be able to inspire the journeyman to offer ideas. With whom do you want to share this experience? If the collaboration is satisfying, a crew should work harmoniously. If there is friction between the director and the director of photography, opposing camps will emerge which will damage company morale. This is not to say that fractious, bickering crews can't make fine movies. It's just a little harder on the nerves.

Several weeks prior to principal photography a director of photography is brought on to shape the look of the film. In addition, he or she shoots camera, wardrobe and make-up tests. The director of photography brings in a first assistant cameraman, a gaffer and a grip. These three crew members in turn hire their own support team. The first assistant cameraman hires a second and a clapper/loader. The gaffer hires a team of electricians, and the key grip hires a best boy and a team of as many grips required by the show. The director of photography's crew then builds (creates shelving for the equipment) the interior of the camera, grip and electric trucks, based on an equipment list provided by the director of photography. The production manager buys the stock, which is kept in a refrigerator and transferred as needs be to the camera truck.

The cinematographer is the eye of the director and translates what's in the director's head onto film. The director of photography must shoot the film in a way that matches or enhances the director's vision. If the cinematographer's work is at odds with the director's vision, that person is wrong for the job. The best way to know how well this collaboration will play out is through discussions, examples and storyboards. The visual style of the film should be determined long before a camera is turned on.

If the director is responsible for the acting, and the director of photography for the lighting and camera movement, the art director is responsible for everything else in the frame. Props, sets, wardrobe, make-up and special effects all fall into this department. A production designer is similar, brought on very early to work with the director and director of photography on the look and style of the film. An art director, also an important creative collaborator, is brought on later to affect the look and style chosen by the director.

The art director hires a costume designer, prop master, hair, make-up and set dressers. These department heads then hire their assistants. If construction is required, a team of carpenters and painters will fall in behind a construction coordinator. The art director also secures the services of a storyboard artist who is assigned to the director.

The sound mixer is a two-person team consisting of the recordist and boom operator. It is their job to send to the editing room the best quality production sound.

Responsibilities of the Sound Team

- Record "clean" dialogue

- Match sound perspective with camera angle
- Record sound effects to accompany the shot
- Record room tone
- Record additional sounds
- Record the scene so it will cut smoothly (sound consistency)
- Keep accurate sound reports

The "A" team is made up of the director and department heads. A director also establishes a personal team composed of the storyboard artist, script supervisor and assistant to the director. The storyboard artist and script supervisor keep the director on track and focused on the continuity of the film and how to send the most effective material to the editing room. The assistant to the director manages creature comforts and personal matters, which frees the director to concentrate on the task at hand.

The "B" team is the second unit, which is composed of a cinematographer/operator, first assistant camera, clapper/loader and an additional second assistant director. During principal photography, a second unit might be assigned to shoot second camera in an action sequence, or shots that do not require principal actors. These shots may have been assigned to a second unit on the original schedule or may be slop shots left over from a shoot the "A" team couldn't finish. These types of shots would include pick-ups, inserts, drive-bys, establishing exterior shots, etc.

A few more individuals play an important role in the life of the crew. Since an army moves on its stomach, a caterer makes a valid contribution to the success of the film. Good hot food, and plenty of it, goes a long way to grease the wheels of a production. It is inevitable that the crew will grumble about the food. A caterer cannot please everyone. And although the director does not hire the caterer, and is probably too absorbed in directing to pay much attention to diet, this department plays its role in the outcome of the picture.

Moving an army swiftly from one battle to the next is akin to the role the transportation captain plays on a movie set. A director needs the company when shooting at a location, to get in as many shots as possible, or certainly the minimum to cover a scene. Errors on the part of the transportation captain can cause delays, which ultimately affect the director's daily production goal.

The post-production department heads are the editor and composer. They are welcome participants during both pre-production and production, although they become most active after the picture has completed shooting. As major contributors to the film's outcome, their involvement is encouraged as soon as they are hired.

The editor cuts the film. Editing is the shaping and assembling of each scene in the order indicated by the screenplay. An editor's technical goal is to stitch the film together seamlessly so the audience does not notice the editing. Artistically the editor makes the film flow to a rhythm that allows the audience to follow and enjoy the story.

The screenplay, the shot material, and comments from the director during dailies guide the editor. With this information the editor usually makes a first cut of the film during principal photography. The creative influence an editor has over the final product is as profound as that of any of the department heads, for it is the editor who blends all the efforts into a final piece. In searching out the most exciting elements, all the while keeping the story in mind, an editor may shape a sequence around a specific line of dialogue, an interesting shot, a dynamic sound cue, a beautiful tableau, the twist of a body, the blink of an eye.

The editor has a team to help assemble the film and prepare it for projection. This includes at least one assistant, a sound editor and a mixer. The editor cuts picture and dialogue. When the score has been recorded, the editor will lay in the tracks in their appropriate position. Sound effects and foley (see glossary) work are done by a team of sound effects editors, often contracted off-site. When the picture is finished and all the tracks gathered and matched to the picture, the mixers blend the sounds together onto one track.

The composer creates the music for the picture. It is traditional for a film to have a score. The nature of the picture will dictate the type and amount of music. Some pictures have 50 to 60 minutes of a full philharmonic score; others may use only prerecorded popular songs. Kurosawa's *High and Low* has a brief score of only two minutes. Sometimes there are simply electronic sounds, as in Hitchcock's *The Birds*.

Special effects play an important part in many films. Whether it is the erasing of Gary Sinese's legs in *Forrest Gump*, creating the aliens in *Men in Black* or just making a campfire, a team of experts is called in to produce the desired illusion. Special effects are either real-time effects produced onset (such as wind, rain and fire or prosthetic make-up) or images manipulated, enhanced, or created entirely in post-production.

On-set effects require a special effects supervisor and assistants. Special effects on set sometimes include a stunt, in which case the special effects supervisor and the stunt coordinator collaborate on the shot. Although the director is responsible for every shot and for the safety of the cast and crew, the assistant director takes over the set during complicated stunt/effects shots. The company make-up artist can apply simple special effects make-up. A separate company, contracted for this one aspect of the film, applies complicated make-up and prosthetic designs.

Elaborate live-action shots, such as tank and miniature photography, are executed by a second unit team so as not to take up the time of the first unit. Complicated blue- or green-screen shots often employ the efforts of both the first and second units.

Post-production effects, also called optical and/or digital effects, have become big business (see Chapter 2: Craft). Special effect companies, or houses, have sprung up all over to service the film and television communities. The special effect houses specialize in enhancing and creating images that either cannot be created on set or that are created on a computer. They can enhance the production value of a shot for a fraction of what it would cost in principal photography. A green-screen shot, for example, is executed first on set with the principal actors with the backgrounds added later in post-production.

The publicist is active during production collecting stories and photographs. The stills photographer, equipped with a silent camera, shoots pictures during the shooting, which belong to the production company for publicity purposes. The majority of this material will eventually be part of a grand effort in post-production to create hype for the film and produce a press package. If the director approves, the publicist can arrange for television, radio or print interviews during principle photography while actors are at rest. Though most directors prefer a closed set (see glossary), publicity is ultimately the director's friend when it comes to competing for box office dollars amid the flood of competing pictures. Directors seek to find a balance between creating an atmosphere of intense concentration and efficiency on the one hand, and meeting demands of the publicity department on the other.

To work shoulder to shoulder with someone for long hours, for days on end, requires a degree of camaraderie. Without it, the process can become a chore, and the film could lose its magic. Being professional means having a capacity to work with people you may not like. So choose wisely.

Budget

Call in every favor and every friend in the business and make the best picture you can possibly make.
— Martha Coolidge

There exists a balance between the funds and the schedule required to produce a film or video project. One usually equates a budget with money, but since time is such an important factor in film production, the two are inescapably linked. Therefore budget here refers to these two precious resources.

The majority of the budget is allocated during principal photography. The amount of time one can shoot is based on the funds available, and the funds required depend on the nature of the shoot. A low-budget show must shoot quickly, and a star-driven sci-fi epic comes with a steep price tag.

Upon reading the screenplay in the early pre-production phase of a film, the director estimates the cost of production based on the elements of the script. An experienced director is often spot on, or at least in the ballpark. As a general rule of thumb, budgets can range as follows:

- shoestring is under $250,000
- extremely low budget is under $750,000
- low budget is between $750,000 and $2,000,000
- low medium budget is anywhere between $2,000,000 and $3,500,000
- medium budget is anywhere between $3,500,000 and $7,500,000
- low big budget is anything between $7,500,000 and $18,000,000

- big budget is anything over $18,000,000
- studio picture will almost always be in excess of $35,000,000
- blockbuster means over $50,000,000 to make the appropriate splash
- star-driven puts it in any of the previous five categories

Whether a director is actively involved in months of fundraising or hired mere weeks before principal photography, he or she must understand and approve the budget and schedule of the production. The responsibility for coming in on budget and on time is ultimately that of the director. Budgets and schedules fall under the purview of the production manager and assistant director, but all departments, especially directorial, contribute to shaping the budget and schedule. The final figures and dates are the result of collaboration between all department heads.

Determining the most efficient manner to shoot, which in turn creates an accurate budget, is based on logic and common sense. Factors such as weather, human foibles and availability can foil even the best-laid plans. A production budget and schedule remain in a state of flux until the assistant director shouts out on the last day, "That's a wrap!"

Once a ballpark figure is balanced with the script and the director's designs, that money needs to be secured.

Green Light

Entertainment venture capital is high-risk. Investors looking for a safe bet seek opportunities in areas other than entertainment. But investors interested in risk, and a potentially high return on their money, do well to look at entertainment projects. So we can establish from the start that people willing and interested in financing films are gamblers with the capacity to lose.

The only safe thing is to take a chance.
— Mike Nichols

Commercial film financing comes from the four corners of the earth: studios, independent production companies, private investors and pre-sales. Noncommercial film financing includes all these sources plus private and government grants.

The Hollywood studios are the major film financiers in America. The eight studios are Universal, MGM/UA, Paramount, Disney, Sony, Warner Bros., Fox and the newest member, DreamWorks. Each of these studios has divisions dedicated to specific genres. Disney, for example, has one division for G-rated youth product (Walt Disney Studios), one for PG-rated shows (Touchstone) and another for R-rated adult fare (Miramax). These studios have deep pockets into which they dig to finance films.

If one sets up a picture at a studio, raising money is never a question. Instead, the questions a studio will ask include:

- Should we make the film?
- Can the screenplay be improved?
- How can we attract the biggest stars?
- How much should we spend?

Once the studio is satisfied with the answers, the project is given a "green light," the equivalent of full financing, or an adequate budget. The project is then overseen by several producers (some of whom are chosen by the studio) and studio executives, whose responsibility is to see that the best picture is made for the budget allocated.

Studios function by developing and producing dynamic films that can be appreciated by both domestic and foreign audiences. They are compelled to make a certain number of films a year to keep their distribution pipeline filled. Since finding good screenplays is a challenge, and making any film a major enterprise, studios may supplement their own production units with outside product known as pick-ups.

When a studio finds a picture in pre-production, production or post-production that they want to own, they "pick-it-up." At whatever stage this occurs, the budget will be increased on a pick-up to accommodate the new owners. It is also a moment when a nonunion or nonsignatory picture must go union, as all studios are signatory to the film production unions and guilds. The feature film *Buffy the Vampire Slayer* was in pre-production when Fox picked it up, at which point the budget jumped from five to eight million. The studios have film buyers on staff who comb festivals, foreign territories, and screenings for finished films seeking distribution. If a studio decides to purchase a finished product, they will act simply as distributors, putting the film into the market and sharing the proceeds with the producers. Often the film requires some enhancements, a new score, a different ending, etc. The studio will arrange for these alterations and deduct the costs from the purchase price and/or the first proceeds.

Studios today are beholden to shareholders, so their tally sheet at the end of a fiscal year should ideally be in the black. Red ink heralds sweeping management changes. There is no way to guarantee a profit to the investors. A studio calculates that if it sends 15 pictures into the marketplace in a given year, a certain percentage may be blockbusters, some may turn a modest profit, some will break even and some will tank. If, when all the profits and losses are added up, the studio returns a figure greater than the prime rate to its stockholders, they can claim financial health.

Studios take on projects in three tiers: development, packaged or finished product. Most studio executives are constantly on the lookout for ideas, pitches, screenplays and literature that might make a good film. It might come from the reader in the story department or the president of the studio. Only the president and a handful of vice presidents have the authority to green-light a film. The remainder of the workforce nudges what it feels are viable properties up the chain of command to someone who can give a final yes or no.

Each studio has a development or story department staffed by readers and executives whose job it is to find material and develop it into viable screenplays. These departments have budgets with which to buy verbal pitches, magazine and newspaper articles, treatments, books and first-draft screenplays. These works are put into "development" where the material is turned into a screenplay either by the original writer, a staff writer, or an outside author assigned to the project. Several writers may work on the material until it is either passed up the ladder or buried.

Packaging is a practice wherein a producer, director and/or agency approach a studio with a project that comprises a viable screenplay, a reputable director, and actors of note. From a creative standpoint, a studio chief can immediately see the potential in having these key elements already in place. The material has excited the talent and if it is something the studio would like to make, a green light can be given on very short notice. The nature of the story, and the bottom-line figure of the budget, coupled with the popularity of the director and/or actors, greatly lowers the studio's financial risk.

A package is solidified only after a deal has been successfully negotiated. The studio may question some of the elements in the package and may ask for adjustments to be made, such as a smaller budget, a stronger director, or a different cast. Once these issues have been resolved, contracts are signed and the project can go directly into production.

Independent Production Companies produce films in most major cities. They may make only one or two films a year. They may also make commercials and industrials to help finance the riskier films. Some companies have output deals with studios, while others have access to funds from banks and local investors. These companies cannot manufacture large-scale productions like the studios, so they gravitate to inexpensive genres such as romantic comedy, drama and character-driven films.

Private investors are individuals eager to gamble in the glamorous arena of film. Others see films as a viable high-risk investment. A certified public accountant (CPA) or personal business manager may be in an ideal position to advise clients to take a risk on a film project. If successful, the clients may become veteran investors. Some investors are interested in a career change to film producer. In exchange for financing a picture, an investor can claim the title of producer and learn the ropes on the job.

Presales occur when a producer takes the package directly to markets. The producer will sell the rights for distribution in that territory before the film is actually made. These territories include domestic theatrical, foreign theatrical (country by country if need be), television, cable, DVD, airlines, and the military. A producer can then discount the contracts from these distribution outlets and borrow the funds directly from one of the many banks that specialize in film financing.

To bridge financing should the budget fall short, one can defer certain fees. Any of the principals, such as the director, producer, writer or lead actor, can be contracted to receive some of their salary during production with the balance of their fee when (and if) the film generates a profit. For example, should each of the four principals negotiate a fee of $100,000, and then defer half their salary, the production would either gain $200,000, or it would need $200,000 less than called for in the budget. Once the film is sold, the deferments are paid out to the principals.

Crews can also be tapped to receive some of their salary in a deferred position. Should crew members be asked to work for less than their quote, they consider their labor as an investment in the picture. The difference in the salary figure taken at the back end is usually increased by

10 percent to compensate for the risk. On some pictures, cast and crew might also be granted net points, which is a risk one step beyond a deferment.

A director appreciates that the script is, in part, currency. An expensive sequence can be shot with less coverage than originally planned, and the money saved redistributed to areas of the budget that balloon beyond expectation. For example, say the director and production manager schedule a sequence to be shot over three days at a cost of $100,000 a day. Before the sequence is shot, a previous scene goes over schedule by a day, adding $100,000 to the budget. The director can go over budget or, by reducing a three-day sequence to two, attempt to even out the expenses.

Schedule

A schedule is determined only after an analysis of the numerous details necessary to realize the screenplay. The budget and the director's estimate of how long it will take to shoot any given sequence shape this appraisal. The breakdowns created by the production team, plus the director's breakdowns, storyboards and floor plans, make up the formula used to create a production schedule.

Ten Key Steps to Preparing a Budget
1. Decide on the scale of the project
2. Determine the shooting schedule
3. Study the script
4. Above the line
5. Key rates
6. Build vs. practical
7. Departmental budgets
8. Local vs. distant location
9. Post-production
10. The cost of money

Whether the budget is big or small a director bears in mind five key dates that will dictate the framework of the schedule and in turn the budget. They are first day of principal photography, last day of principal photography, director's cut, mix and the release date.

A start date is the same as a green light. On such and such day, principal photography will commence. All the days in preparation, even if the project is a "go" or "green lit," are actually "yellow" lights. The production proceeds with caution. Occasionally a picture is aborted prior to principle photography. But once principle photography commences, shutting down or abandoning a project is rare.

Working backward from the start date, the director then has an idea how much preparation time is available. There is a direct correlation between the amount of pre-production time to the quality of the end product. If directors are given a huge budget for a complicated film but told in the same breath they must start in two days' time, the shooting will be much less productive than if the director were given adequate preparation time. If one calculates at least a week of preparation for every week of principal photography, then a ten-week shoot should begin a minimum of two and a half months prior to the start date. Now you have a pre-production schedule. In fact, most productions generate a pre-pre-production schedule as well. Rather than wait for the company to assemble, a small team consisting of director, director of photography, production designer, production manager and location manager outline the concept of the shoot. What city will it shoot in? Locations or studios? This is the time to nail down the look of the film.

The start date reveals when cast and crew members might be available. As discussed in the previous two chapters, availability and negotiated fees determine who will act in and work on a particular film. If an actor is not available by your start date, you may want to exercise an option to postpone the shoot.

The budget dictates the number of shooting days. This calculation sets a stop date for principal photography. A low-budget show must shoot quickly, perhaps six-day weeks for three to four weeks. A mid-sized budget might afford the director a six-week shoot. The larger the budget, the more time to shoot. From this shooting schedule a formula is applied to determine the number of pages to be shot each day.

There is an axiom in the film industry that one page of screenplay equals one minute of screen time. Although not precise, it's a fine way to approximate the schedule. If the screenplay is 120 pages long with a 30-day shooting schedule, then the director must average four pages a day. Some days the schedule will call for one page to be shot, and on other days the director can bang out seven pages. The schedule will ultimately be based on these figures. If, for example, the director is scheduled to shoot a total of 12 pages in the first three days of the shoot, but manages to only shoot six, the producers can calculate that a 30-day shoot may well end up a 60-day shoot. If the production budget suggests a shooting day to cost on the average $200,000, then the overage can be projected to be in the neighborhood of $6,000,000. Not good.

The director agrees, prior to the first day of principal photography, to meet the schedule. The completion bond company demands the director sign off on the production schedule, making a legal commitment to the dates. The director has had a major hand in the shaping of the production schedule, and the director's job, once shooting starts, is to "make the pages." This refers to the director's responsibility to adhere to the production schedule. Any deviation from the schedule can result in overages, violation of turnaround, and schedule conflicts. Besides doing their best to produce a good film, directors are duty bound to "make the pages." This is not an exact science; some days will go slowly, others more quickly. A director's primary duty is to make a good film but to do so in a responsible manner; otherwise there is the possibility of being removed from the picture. Also not good.

Directors function in what is known as the Entertainment Business. The accent is on the word *business*. While directors often state they are shooting a movie, not a schedule, every decision is influenced in some way by their responsibility to the budget and schedule. Fiscal negligence is a one-way ticket to obscurity. Both noted directors Eric Von Stroheim and Michael Cimino fell victim to their own indulgences, and their careers suffered as a result.

The First Day

Day 1 is very light. An easy first day gives the cast and crew time to build up a momentum and allows for the kind of initial mistakes that are inevitable.

Day 1 is an average day. Every day is important, so a day that has an average amount of pages to shoot is a fair day. This choice does not treat the first day as anything special.

Day 1 is heavy. A deliberately heavy day in which the cast and crew have to hit the ground running is an opportunity to galvanize the company. Dead weight becomes obvious very quickly.

Every aspect of the production is broken down onto breakdown sheets, which are then transferred to a computerized or manual strip board.

The strip board schedule is a system of strips, each one representing a scene and grouped together to make up each day's principal photography. These days are then arranged into weeks, and with one glance the director has an overview of the entire production schedule. Each strip contains encoded information culled from the breakdown sheets relevant to the scene, such as which characters are on camera, whether the scene is day or night, interior or exterior, and the length of the scene in screenplay pages.

The assistant director, production manager or producer lays out a strip board schedule for the first time continuity. This first schedule is in screenplay order; scene #2 follows scene #1, scene #3 after scene #2, etc. If scenes can be scheduled consecutively in this way, so much the better. Continuity affords the actors a direct through line of development. It is easier to make discoveries when actors build one beat upon another.

Most film schedules are calculated not in script order. Scene #4 may follow scene #93 and scene #62a may follow scene #4, etc. This one key fact spotlights the importance of the director. As the sole audience member on set, it is the director's job to manage the puzzle of the jumbled screenplay while shooting so that it can be pieced together into a seamless whole.

The two dominant factors in calculating a schedule are cast and locations, as these are the most sizable budget chunks. The trick to an efficient schedule (and resulting budget) is to "shoot out" or group together in the production schedule "big ticket" or costly items such as actors and locations.

Take, for example, a scene set in a library. Scenes #8 and #31, each five pages, are both played in this location. The numbers tell us that the scenes are set far apart in the film. Constructing and dressing a library set is more expensive than locating an existing library and renting it for several days. Despite the administrative hassles with local officials to shut down a public building, eventually the proper permits will be secured and a fee negotiated. The day of the shoot will require time to protect the floors and bring in the cables from the generator for the lights. Once the lights are roughed in, shooting can commence.

When scene #8 is shot, the lights are reset, if necessary, for scene #31. When both scenes are successfully in the can, the location is restored to an as good as, if not better, condition than when they found it. The finding, securing, swooping in, setting lights, shooting and quick exit is a typical major effort in the making of a film. This is "shooting out" the location. Avoid doing it twice if possible. The time to set up and wrap out might be in the range of 4 to 8 hours, depending on the nature of the production. To go in for a second time means 8 to 16 hours' time not shooting.

The next calculation in this library exercise would be to examine the availability of the actors. If the two scenes require different high-paid actors, it may be necessary to shoot one scene with one actor and return to the library several weeks later to shoot the other actor's scene. One could lay out a similar exercise beginning with a single actor's schedule. Hired for three days as a guest star at great expense, it would behoove the production to "shoot out the actor" rather than pay for additional shooting days. What the powers that be ultimately decide is which of the options is most cost effective: to hire the actor for additional days or to return to a location.

Other "big ticket" items in film production, besides actors and locations, include crowd scenes (extras), studios, elaborate stunts, and green screen. In addition, there is specialized film equipment, such as a helicopter, crane or underwater housing unit, all of which can also be grouped together. Crowd scenes, especially period sequences, are a logistical challenge, best executed when the crowds are dressed, gathered, directed and shot within a single time frame. Stunts, special effects and specialized film equipment are all better utilized when grouped together on the schedule.

Soundstage shooting should also be grouped, if possible, because the company can save money by dropping all the trucks, campers and lighting package. The soundstage provides these three items, so it makes no sense to pay for them twice.

Each strip on the strip board is color-coded to indicate one of four major shooting locales: interior-day, interior-night, exterior-day, exterior-night. They are usually white, red, blue, green, but any combination will do. Strips may also be color-coded, to identify specialty scenes, such as stunts or magic hour so they jump out at the viewer.

The four basic shooting periods are often laid out on the board in groupings. Should the show require six exterior nights, it is best to shoot them out as a unit. If a company is shooting exterior day, they wrap at around 6 P.M. If the next day's shoot is an exterior night, the company cannot be called until 6 P.M. the following day. This leaves a gap of 24 hours between shooting days, an inefficient use of time. The same thing would be true in the switch from nights to days. Six exterior nights make a full week, and there is no loss of time if the company starts their week at 6 P.M. on a Monday and ends it at 6 A.M. the following Saturday.

Calculating the most efficient use of time between shooting days introduces the concept of "turnaround." Between the wrap time on one day, and the call time for the next, a certain number of hours must elapse; a minimum of 8 hours for crew and 12 for actors. These are union regulations and are also common sense. To work a crew hard and then ask them to begin another long day without proper rest will only hurt the film in the long run (see Chapter 5: Health). One can examine the few catastrophic deaths on set, such as Brandon Lee in *The Crow* or Vic Morrow in *Twilight Zone: The Movie* and see that shooting long hours, late into the night, contributed to the tragic lapse in safety.

If night shoots cannot be avoided, an option is to consider "splits," wherein the crew is called at noon and wrapped at midnight. This affords the director a half day of light for day: exterior and a half day of night for night: exterior.

Turnaround affects the entire schedule. It can either be assessed at the beginning of the scheduling process or when an on-the-spot adjustment is made during principal photography. This is why it is so important for the director to understand the mechanics of a strip board. Its one thing to study and adjust the board during a pre-production meeting. It is quite another when a schedule needs to be altered during a shoot for an unplanned event, such as an illness or loss of location. In the flurry of planning a schedule adjustment during shooting, it is imperative to read the board accurately and as a whole shoot. The ripple effect of moving one strip can make an entire schedule come apart. Actors and locations have been contractually lined up for specific dates. Sets have to be built and locations prerigged for lights. Moving one date may adversely affect another. Often decisions to alter the schedule have to be made at lightning speed, and mistakes can be costly.

The camera and art department also have turnaround issues to factor into the strip board. A big interior set piece may require extensive prerigging in order to hang lights. An interior location may need days for elaborate redressing. To jump to these locales prematurely will cost the company time while the crew adjusts the rigging or dresses the set. In other words, it is one thing to nail down a location and another to prepare that location for shooting. If a location is good to shoot as-is, the company can jump there on a moment's notice; otherwise the prep time is as important a calculation as actor or location availability.

If a tight turnaround cannot be avoided, one option is to consider scheduling a day: exterior prior to an interior location that necessitates rigging or dressing. If the sun cooperates, shooting outside eliminates the need for lights. Giant pieces of silk are placed overhead for close shots, to diffuse and guarantee even light. The lighting crew and set dressers can be excused from the exterior shoot (only mother nature can properly light and dress a forest) and jump to the interior location to pre-rig.

Finally, the schedule is informed by any fixed dates inherited by the production. A unique location may be available only on a specific date. Actors are contracted to begin on or about a specific date (within a week) to allow for some fine-tuning of the first day of principal photography. A producer should avoid, if possible, hiring an actor with a "stop" date connected to the contract. A stop date informs the producers that on a particular day the actor has the right to leave the shoot and to move on to a prior commitment. Stop dates are fixed on the schedule and become irksome should your show begin to go over schedule, for the actor must be gone on the stop date. It is not unusual for an actor, especially one signed for the "run-of-the-show," to negotiate a day off for a pre-arranged commitment such as an awards ceremony, wedding, bar mitzvah, etc.

One of the main reasons Hollywood exists in sunny California is because there are approximately 350 good shooting days. Despite being subject to weather, exteriors bring with them great expanse and beauty of nature, which look spectacular on film. François Truffaut once said the two things that look best on film are a train and the snow. Only through experience can a director learn the complications, challenges and joys of shooting exteriors. Rain, heat, cold, clouds and the sun all call for patience and some luck.

In an ideal world, a director will first shoot out all exteriors, then move on to interiors. If the weather holds and the director gets all exterior material in the can, then when the company moves indoors, the weather is no longer a factor. Weather is one of the great unknowns on a film shoot, unless the shoot is entirely interior. Film production companies have a great deal of control over their environment, but none over the weather. Wind, rain, clouds, even sun can cause delays.

Rain is tricky because it often rains for a short time and then stops.

An exterior scene can be shot during a light drizzle without looking too wet. In fact, unless backlit, rain is practically invisible to the camera. Barring a downpour, the production manager calls the company to the location as if they plan to shoot. Upon arrival, a judgment is made between the department heads: to remain at the location or run to the cover set. Skipping a day's shooting is not an option.

A good rule of thumb when preparing a budget and schedule is to identify, if possible, a cover set. This is an interior scene always dressed and ready to go at a moment's notice. Ideally it should be a half or full day's photography, requiring only principal actors. The cover set is then placed at the end of the schedule. If the scheduled scene for the day is an exterior and the weather proves inclement, the production manager can send the company to the cover set to avoid going behind schedule.

Interiors may sometimes be cramped and become quite hot from the lights, but directors gain considerable control over their environment shooting inside, including light, sound, even time of day. At night, high-intensity lamps color balanced for daylight can be placed outside windows to simulate the sun. Conversely, windows can be tented with black velour to shut out sunlight to shoot a night: interior during the daytime, or appropriate lighting (simulated daylight or moonlight) can be placed inside the tent so the time of day is constant.

The time of year one shoots informs the schedule. During daylight savings, days are short, so a day: exterior scene may be over by 5 P.M. Some locales are known for rainy seasons, hot spells, Santa Ana winds, etc. Francis Ford Coppola is most likely an expert, after shooting *Apocalypse Now*, predicting the monsoon season in the Philippines.

Always scout a location for light and sound issues. If the company needs to shoot exteriors in Canada or Israel, the quality of the light will be radically different. The traffic sounds at 8 A.M. are quite different from those at 11 A.M. The longer the location is examined, the more it becomes a part of the creative process. Locations have character and idiosyncrasies, so a director should make use of these properties.

When the assistant director calls the company to a location for a full day's shooting there is no move, only an arrival and departure, a wrap in and wrap out. When there is less than a day's work at one location, the company must relocate to shoot more material to make up a full day's work. Travel during a shooting day is time consuming. Moving the company from one location to another in a timely manner is a logistical challenge. A skilled location manager can move the team quickly and quietly, truck by truck, car by car, so as to make for the most efficient use of time. Keep the number of company moves to a bare minimum when laying out the strip board. If a company move takes an average of two hours, every move is two hours out of the shooting schedule. Two moves a day is four hours, and four moves you might as well stay home.

Creating the Schedule

- Start with any fixed dates of which you are aware. These will become the anchors around which you must work.
- Group your locations together, but try to place the exteriors first.
- Factor in the actors' schedules.
- Factor in the day and night schedule if appropriate. Remember that 12 hours of turnaround time is required between days and nights. Use the weekend to make this transition.
- Identify any other special adjustments your project demands, such as special effects or crowd sequences.

All the issues addressed so far have had major impact on the schedule. Children, animals and crowds have minor but noteworthy consequences for a production schedule. Child actors have many contractual issues by which the company must abide. Union regulations allow children to work only so many hours at a time, depending on age; babies up to 2 years old can only be on set for 50 minutes at a time (infant twins are often cast to double the time the director can shoot), and toddlers for an hour. Child actors 5 to 8 years old can only work 20 minutes at a time, must have three hours of schooling a day by a registered welfare worker, and one-hour rest. Actors between 9 and 18 years old can work longer, do not require the rest period, but also need schooling if they are not graduated from high school. Some welfare workers will allow the company to "bank" hours, so if the child is schooled one day for six hours, the following day he or she can shoot without schooling.

The assistant director knows from the screenplay and the director's shooting plan how much time might be required for shooting children, which is reflected in the schedule, in addition to the above-mentioned rules and regulations. Because children, even professional child actors, are unpredictable, a conservative assistant director will pad the schedule in case the child is uncooperative. As one can imagine, some kids are a dream to work with, others a nightmare. Cast both the child and parent wisely.

Animals bring with them a unique set of challenges. Just as a parent or social worker chaperones a child actor, animals are attended by trainers. The key to working with animals is to have them trained prior to shooting to do whatever is required by the script. The trainer is hired early in pre-production and the specifics required by the animal defined by the director. The trainer then goes away and coaches the animal accordingly. The example in Chapter 2 was the multiple pigs employed in the movie *Babe*. Most animals can do one or two tricks on command. Too many bits of direction may be confusing to the animal and frustrating to the director (who needs to shoot and move on), the trainer (responsible for the animal's performance) and consequently the schedule.

Controlled crowd scenes lend credibility to a film. During the weekday, a street, train station, or school hallway swarms with people. The assistant director controls a team of people designated background extras to fill the frame as in real life. Extras require make-up, wardrobe and direction to be an integral part of the scene. They are moved from point to point during any given take and must match that same action for each additional camera angle. On days when large numbers of extras are necessary, the assistant director will put on auxiliary assistant directors to control the crowd of extras. Supplementary make-up and wardrobe personnel are also hired to ensure the extras are prepared in time for photography.

A DVD playing home movies of the characters in the film has to be shot prior to principal photography. Stills of the happy family that cover the grand piano are taken, developed and framed as props in pre-production. Therefore a director is prepared to shoot material during pre-production, which plays a part in principal photography.

Second unit and swing crews are two budget categories worth consideration to save time and guarantee ample material for the editing room. A second unit (see Chapter 6: Craft) is sometimes considered a luxury, especially on a low-budget show. But the time saved and the extra material generated by a second unit is worth consideration. A big-budget show may have a second unit available throughout the shoot. If the budget doesn't allow for a second unit, the director can ask one be hired for at least a few days or a week to assist the first unit. If this camera can be employed both as a second camera and also as a second unit, the director can ask this unit to shoot material without principal actors, for example, drive-bys, inserts, long shots, establishing shots, beauty

shots, etc. Every one of these shots done by a second unit relieves the
first unit to spend more time on scenes involving principals.

A second unit (and often up to six cameras) is always used for stunts
to shoot a second angle so the stunt is performed as few times as possible. Large set pieces, such as musical numbers, benefit from a second camera. In both these cases, it is the third and fourth camera that becomes
the luxury. Many shows opt to employ two cameras. Often the two cameras are placed side by side to get a medium and close shot simultaneously. However, the more one separates the cameras the greater difficulty
to light. It can be faster to light for one camera than two. A calculation
to consider is whether the cost of the additional camera(s) saves "X"
number of set-ups per day.

Swings crews are a team of electricians or set dressers hired to light
or dress the set the night before the company is to shoot a big scene.
This is not a luxury if the money spent on the swing crew is less than
the approximate cost of having the production unit take the time to light
and dress the set on a day of principal photography. If a 10-hour day's
work is calculated at $50,000, then one hour is $5,000. If a swing crew
costs the company $10,000, but saves four hours of set up time, the com-
pany saves approximately $10,000.

Once a show starts, money flows quickly to pay for production.
Seven buffers against bankruptcy include:

- Script — Revising and condensing the script during principal
  photography, as long as it does not change the essence of the
  story, is capital available to the director.
- Cast — Hiring a dedicated and professional cast eliminates some
  concerns about making the budget and schedule.
- Crew — Hiring a dedicated and professional crew eliminates some
  concerns about making the budget and schedule.
- Post-production — Borrowing from post-production to pay for
  production is one method of maintaining an adequate production budget, the results of which are that something planned for
  post-production, such as opticals or score, may be compromised.
- Insurance — Always secure a healthy insurance package.
- Completion Bond — Protection from disaster.
- Points — If necessary, the creative team and/or general partners in
  a limited partnership can sell net points (see glossary) to infuse
  cash to the budget.

Film- and video-making generates mounds of paperwork. Production paperwork conveys a road map that accurately promotes the director's vision (see Chapter 7: Command). These documents include screenplay, budget, contracts, breakdowns, storyboards, production schedule, "day out of days," call sheets and production reports.

The production schedule is informed by all these documents, particularly the last three items. The "day out of days" is a useful grid that identifies exactly when characters are scheduled to work. Each day of the production is listed on the horizontal with the characters arranged vertically on the left. When this grid is completed, any production executive can see when the actors are employed at a glance. This tool is particularly helpful when altering the schedule, to assure each actor's contract is respected or, if need be, adjusted to accommodate the new schedule.

Call sheets outline the plan for the next shooting day. Handed out at wrap to the cast and crew, the call sheet includes the place and time each department (including actors) must arrive. The call sheet identifies many specifics related to the shooting day, including the scenes and the order in which they are planned to be shot. A map to the location and important telephone numbers in case of an emergency are printed on the back of the call sheet.

If the call sheet suggests what will happen, the production report tells what did happen. This document identifies when the cast and crew actually arrived, when the first shot was executed, how much footage was exposed, whether any insurance claims were made and generally sums up the shooting day. Producers and studio executives read these reports in lieu of being on set all day. This summary tells the producers how well the production is proceeding.

A director must always make the day, read the board carefully, and remember that things change. Luis Buñuel said when making *Los Olvidados*, "It was made in 21 days, right on schedule, as usual. Where deadlines are concerned, I've never missed a single one, nor has it taken me more than three or four days to do the editing."

Post-Production

The budget for post-production is what remains after the expense of principal photography. If considerable sums have been shifted from the post-production budget to production to ensure principal photography can be completed, post-production then also becomes an additional fundraising period. With many low-budget shows, a cut of the film on tape is shown to potential distributors and/or financing agencies with the hope they will provide the necessary finishing funds.

Unless a director has final cut, a contractual date is specified for the delivery of a "director's cut," usually several months after the last day of principal photography. On this date the producers decide to either continue editing the film or to lock picture and prepare the soundtracks. The director keeps an eye on this date to ensure the print screened for the producers is as complete as possible. To screen a cut of a film without music to the untrained eye can be a choppy start-and-stop experience. It is advisable to take some time out of the editing schedule to create a temporary music track so the audience (test screenings and producer screenings) gains a sense of the flow of the picture. Nothing binds a picture together more successfully than music.

The composer's duty is to interpret the director's emotional intent through music.

So, it becomes an exercise in futility if you write something that does not express the film as the director wishes. It's still their ball game. It's their show. I think any successful composer learns how to dance around the director's impulses. You have to write a good score that you feel good about. At least, you're supposed to. But, if the director hates it, it ain't going to be in the movie! I'm trying to interpret the film through the director's head, but it all comes out through me. So, a composer is kind of like a psychic medium.

— Danny Elfman

Once the picture has been locked, the sound work, including the score, begins. It is common to wait for a locked picture before building the soundtrack because there may be dozens of tracks, each of which need to be edited to match any cuts in the picture. When the tracks are finalized, they are all blended together in the mix. A mix date is reserved in advance because sound mixing takes several weeks, is costly, and sound-mixing studios get booked quickly. The director stays on the picture even after the director's cut until the final print has been made.

There is a minimum of four weeks between locking picture and a sound mix, and a minimum two weeks between the sound mix and the first print. Depending on the schedules of the facilities the company has booked, a final print is delivered only after all the requisite sound and optical work has been completed. Opticals include titles, fades, dissolves, wipes and visual transitions. Elaborate opticals such as a superimpositions, lap dissolves, wet gate blow-ups, step printing and matte shots take considerably longer to finalize. Wedge tests are judged to determine the proper exposure, and consideration is given to the grain in the shots immediately preceding and following the optical.

Post-production can be particularly lengthy if the show involves complicated green-screen and CGI (computer generated images) shots. Both making a computer generated image, such as a running dinosaur, and blending it in with the background and principal players take great care and finesse. The computer has become a valuable tool in filmmaking in that it so easily blends elements together in a frame to satisfy the image required by the story. These opticals are, however, costly and time consuming, though the results can be stunning.

Finally there is a release date. At one end of the spectrum, a film can be rushed through all the production and post-production phases only to then sit on a shelf and wait a year to be released. At the other extreme, a film is rushed through to get a release print to theaters as soon as possible. This is called delivering a wet print, as it has hardly had time to dry before its first screening.

Budget

Just as the screenplay is the blueprint or plan for how to shoot the movie, the budget is the blueprint or plan for how the funds will be spent to realize the film. Screenplay and budget are joined at the hip and are almost identical in length (120 pages), weight (about 6 ounces) and importance. A director with a budget of $1 million and a screenplay that can't be made for under $50 million is as absurd as a director with a $50 million budget and a screenplay with two actors set entirely on a park bench. Shooting a film is analogous to starting a company, manufacturing a product, and closing the company all within a twelve-month period. After all, it is the entertainment *business*, so a producer needs a business plan, and part of that plan is the budget.

A budget is divided into two sections, above-the-line and below-the-line. Above-the-line refers to costs associated with hiring the principals: director, producer(s), writer(s) and actors. It also includes the cost of purchasing and/or developing the screenplay. Everything else — the costs associated with the manufacturing of the picture — is below-the-line. Moneys allocated to the principals are paid out in flat fees, while salaries for all others are paid out weekly.

The ratio between above-the-line and below-the-line costs on a low-budget show is comfortable at 1:2. On a $3 million picture, approximately $1 million will be allocated to the principals and $2 toward the making of the film. Since the salaries of the principals are a fixed cost, the 1:2 ratio can be adjusted accordingly. If the cost for principals jumps to $2 million, the total cost of the picture will be more likely in the neighborhood of $6 million. The ratio is closer to 1:1 on a studio or big-budget picture. This is because the stars' salaries, entourage and support system are so expensive. In the film *Changing Lanes*, the above-the-line was $40 million and the below-the-line was $40 million.

This ratio compels good agents to make a deal for their directing client on a sliding percentage scale. A 5 percent of the below-the-line budget fee means the $500,000 originally offered in the first budget scenario leaps to $2,000,000 in the second. Novice directors can (and should) also make a jump when the budget balloons, but their deals often have a cap or ceiling.

The script and schedule dictate the below-the-line. The producer or production manager makes an educated guess based on experience and knowledge of current prices. The screenplay dictates the number of scenes to be shot, the number of actors to be employed, the nature of the locations, and the parameters of the art department. A period film has needs different from those of a contemporary show. An action picture demands stunts not required in a romantic comedy. Horror films take advantage of atmospheric sets and night photography, while a comedy is often bright and colorful.

Directors contribute concepts that affect the budget, such as the look or style of the picture, a coverage plan, film stocks, numbers of extras, etc. They then ask if the picture is best served by practical locations or sets or a combination of the two. Practical locations need to be secured, traveled to, and redressed, and are often confining. They are also less expensive than building sets. Sets shot on a sound stage are easily controlled, require less travel, and afford a crew plenty of room for dressing, lighting and camera moves. Sound stages are sound proof. And they are expensive.

Veteran directors can promote an efficient budget (and schedule) by discerning approximately how much can be shot in any given situation. The basic routine is to call the cast and crew at a specific time, rehearse and light for the first scene, shoot it and then move on. Each new set or location requires transition time, especially if the company has to pick up and move any significant distance. All the time setting up, traveling, cabling in and wrapping out is time the director is not shooting. Experience allows directors to calculate how much shooting can be accomplished in a given day.

Often a budget is created, then a schedule, then the budget reallocated, then the schedule adjusted, so on and so forth. As the schedule begins to materialize, so too does an accurate budget. A director likes to complete the picture on time and on budget. Although this concept has little to do with the quality of the film, the stakes are so high in the film business that a reputation for fiscal responsibility is an asset.

A film production is protected from financial disaster in a number of ways. These include the contingency fund, insurance, completion bond, as well as script modification. A contingency fund is a sum of money, approximately 10 percent of the budget, added to the overall production budget in case of cost overruns and production problems. This padding to the budget allows for fluctuations during production. Some production managers go so far as to add a contingency figure to each budget category, in addition to an overall contingency. This money, which in essence is used to cover unexpected expenses, is inevitably spent during production. An expression in movie budgeting circles is that often money is robbed from Peter to pay Paul. This means that shuffling funds from one area of the budget, whether it be contingency funds or moneys assigned to create the score, to another is merely a case of ensuring the production does not slow or shut down, and that as much money as possible goes up on the screen.

With a studio picture, the rule is the higher the budget, the lower the contingency percentage. The entire budget is provided by the studio, and the executives who approve the picture do not want it to come in under budget because if the picture comes in under budget, then the money saved could have been spent on other projects. The fact is the studio itself is the financial guarantor. This is why Cimino's *Heaven's Gate* took such a toll on United Artists when it went considerably over budget.

Every production requires a hefty insurance package. Everything is buffered as much as possible against potential disaster, including the health of all personnel, protection for the equipment from theft and damage, and a guarantee that the negative will survive the laboratory. The director is not involved in the negotiations for insurance. Nor does he or she hire the stunt or the pyrotechnics supervisor. However, it is vitally important that every director knows about insurance, safety, and union regulations.

On top of the insurance package, some productions, especially big-budget independent films, require a completion bond. A completion bond is given by an additional insurance brokerage firm. It guarantees that the film will be made or the money returned to the investors. Should the picture spin out of control to the point where the completion of the picture is in question, the completion bond company is obligated to step in and either pull the plug and return the investment, or complete the film in a timely and efficient manner. Some actors (and directors) have a wild history that causes the studio or production company to take out exorbitant insurance packages with large premiums and hefty deductibles. Landing Robert Downey, Jr., to play the lead in your movie is a good news/bad news scenario. The good news is that he is a brilliant actor; the bad news is he has a "history."

Directors are ever vigilant concerning the quality of the material they are producing. Each scene is a mosaic that must be molded and painted just so. In addition to the shooting, a director should be alert to the cash flow. Although a team of producers and accountants monitors the production reports, money is spent so quickly during principal photography that it takes very little for a show to become a runaway production.

Assuming the management team is honest, and funds are being allocated according to the dictates of the budget, two areas worth special monitoring are cash disbursements in the art department and petty cash. It is difficult to budget the art department accurately during pre-production, as so much occurs during photography that is covered by this department. As a result, the budget for art (which includes construction, set dressing, make-up, hair, wardrobe, props and special effects) can easily balloon. Production managers usually pad the contingency budgets of the art department in anticipation of these overages.

Petty cash is the liquid money doled out by the production office for daily expenses. Hard to calculate, harder still to see how quickly it can inflate, it is still the lifeblood of a production. Overseeing the budget is not the director's primary function, but to ignore it could prove disastrous. All directors should feel comfortable with the daily functioning of the budget and its importance. Understanding finance, cash flows, targets, supply and demand are all part of the world in which, quoting Elia Kazan, "a director knows something about everything."

To shoot the best film possible, directors ask for as much as they can for the production. Starting out with an adequate amount of cash and fighting for more is part of the routine of directing. *Star Wars* was an expensive film and went almost one-third over budget. Once the grosses rolled in, however, no one mentioned the overages.

Income

When the film is finally completed and screened in theaters, money is generated for the participating financiers. The cash received from the public at the box office is termed the "gross." This money travels to the sub-distributors, then to the distributor, then to the production company. Once all these parties have recouped their investments (which includes the cost of production and distribution as well as overhead) the profit is termed the "net." The profit is distributed to any individuals or vendors contracted for net points.

After gross, but before net, there is a financial return position termed *deferments*. This is money stipulated by contracts to be paid to individuals or vendors if the film makes money. It is in a position (called "first position") to be paid out before any other party receives a net profit. For example, a high-paid director of photography may shoot the picture for less than his or her fee and take the balance as a deferment. If the director of photography, despite a quote of $70,000, accepts the picture for $50,000, the remaining $20,000 is owed to the cinematographer *only* if the film generates a profit. If the film doesn't make any money, the balance of the fee remains unpaid.

"When we were doing television," states Terry Gilliam, "we always had big ideas. We did a lot of parodies of films and film directors. I think we were all frustrated by the limitations of the little screen. So, when we set out to do an epic we wanted to have scale, we wanted to have horses.

Of course we didn't get horses, we got coconuts. The success of *Monty Python and the Holy Grail* is due to the fact we didn't have the money to make a mediocre epic. Because given the time and the money we would have been mediocre. But because we didn't, we had to come up with silly ideas, which in the end, proved to be much more interesting."

The budget is important, but it is also critical to remember that no one ever went to a movie because they heard it came in on time and under budget.

◀◀ **5** ▶▶

Health

A director has to pour it on six days a week, twelve hours a day.
— Steven Spielberg

Danger lurks round every corner. If the director falls ill, production stops. This is not true of any cast or crew member. Directing is physically demanding and not for the weak of heart. It requires stamina and a good pair of shoes. Usually energetic, excited and feisty, the director is on set every day. No one has more energy and bounce to their step than the director, who has been preparing to realize the film for a long time. The production can limp along with temporary absences of the lead actor, wardrobe mistress, key grip, assistant director, or the producer. Actors can be shot around, crew members can be replaced and the producer may be absent for days at a time. So it is important for a director to get in shape and stay that way because if the director gets sick, so does the schedule, the budget, and so on.

If, however, the director's absence is due to a serious illness, injury, or death, then the company shuts down while a replacement is sought.

There exists a phenomenon in the film industry referred to as "director's disease." Inexplicable maladies strike many directors during shooting and just as mysteriously disappear when the show wraps. Although many veterans suffer, first timers may be the most susceptible to director's disease. Physical ailments attack the human body during moments of stress and weakness. The first few days of a film shoot may be the most stressful, and after expending so much energy on this first wave of shooting a director might well succumb to weakness and possible ailment.

81

In the introduction, Elia Kazan is quoted as saying a director must be like a baseball outfielder. He was referring to the fact that directors are on their feet all day long. Standing around can be enervating. Poor shoes can sap a director's strength. This is not the first thing that runs through a director's mind when asked to direct a picture, but it should be on the list somewhere. Steven Spielberg, on legs: "Before a picture, the best thing to do is to go to the gym. There comes a time, I swear to you, a time comes when your legs don't work — they're jelly. Your mind is very sharp, but you can't get your body to respond. But you've got to pour it on six days a week, twelve hours a day." Stamina and endurance are directing necessities. There exists a direct correlation between the energy of the director and the material shot. As pictures are shot out of continuity, a director needs to maintain an even pace so the shot material will not fluctuate with the director's own energy levels (see Chapter 8: Pace).

Alfred Hitchcock became ill during the filming of *Psycho*. Saul Bass had asked Hitchcock if he could storyboard the stairway sequence in which Norman Bates, dressed as his mother, kills the detective. Hitchcock said yes, and when he was unable to come to the studio because of his high temperature, he phoned the assistant director and asked him to have Saul Bass film the stairway scene he had designed. "When I looked at the rushes of the scene, I found it was no good," said Hitchcock. "Those shots would have been perfectly all right if they were showing a killer, but they were in conflict with the whole spirit of the scene." Hitchcock recovered quickly and re-shot the scene the next day.

Cocteau was an inspired artist, poet, author, playwright and filmmaker. He was truly an artist who felt compelled to suffer for his art, wearing his maladies on his sleeve.

Cocteau made the classic film *Beauty and the Beast* at the end of World War II. The French government and his financial backers had a difficult time supplying the company with the necessary materials for the film. Electricity was intermittent; equipment was difficult to procure. They could only provide black-and-white 35mm film stock, though Cocteau had wanted to shoot the film in color.

These are typical entries in his diary during the making of the film:

Aug. 26, 1945. I have had to add daily visits to the doctors. As a result of sunburn and bad mosquito bites, I came back from my holiday with two carbuncles on my chest.

Aug. 28, 1945. This afternoon I was almost drunk with fatigue and I got muddled up. My poor head could no longer recall the continuity of the shots.

Aug. 30, 1945. Undoing my dressing I noticed I have a small boil coming. All that I ask is that the boil doesn't get bad before I finish shooting the exteriors.

Sept. 1, 1945. I go to bed utterly exhausted, and so thin that a woman journalist declares: "His face is made of two profiles stuck together."

Directors, along with principal actors, are required to have a physical examination prior to shooting for insurance purposes. The shooting schedule is grueling for a director, and a physical examination gives the producers an idea of the director's fitness. Unfortunately, most physicals are cursory; so a director should be responsible to the production company in analyzing his or her own physical stamina. A responsible director would not knowingly take an assignment if he or she were unfit.

B-12 shots are a common first line of defense against weakness. These shots are administered by the company physician on the first day of principal photography and each week thereafter if need be. There are inoculations one must have should the film require travel outside the United States. Something as common as tourista can fell even the most hardy director. One should be cautious about the food and water in foreign lands.

A regimen of healthy diet, proper rest and regular exercise is the best preventative medicine against illness during a shoot. It is advisable to have written into the director's contract any specific requests to maintain good physical and mental health during the shooting of a film. Sample perks or riders to a director's contract might include:

* access to a gym
* special dietary requirements available at lunch
* laundry service
* a driver

These particulars are itemized because they are not "industry standard" or DGA boilerplate givens. And, if you do not ask for them, you will not get them. To have to do laundry on your day off, or bring in your own yogurt to eat at lunch, takes time away from your rest and concentration.

Just as important as physical health is emotional health. A positive frame of mind is necessary to direct a film. Depression and cloudy thinking go hand in glove with fatigue, poor diet and lack of sleep. Even so, the most debilitating physiological factor may be fear. Fear of failing, fear of not making the pages, fear of not being in control. Directors arriving on set to hear the director of photography ask, "What's the first shot?" often dart to the toilet to throw up. Fear is natural. Vomit if you must, but muster the courage to perform the task at hand. As Cocteau rightly noted: "I was frantic, which is exhausting." Unless you find a way to handle your fears, your directing skills will be lost.

To be sharp, fit and focused and to maintain the energy required of a director over a 10- to 15-hour workday, proper sleep is mandatory. Fitful sleep can cause a director (or anyone, for that matter) to be cranky. He may make bad decisions, which can adversely affect the look, meaning or pace of the film.

Orson Welles is quoted as saying a director should "always get more sleep than your actors." Directors who can cat nap are lucky. With periods of down time common on movie sets, a director can retire to a quiet place for needed rest. Do not hesitate to change your hotel room to avoid sleeping on a heavily trafficked street. Keeping a window open allows fresh air in the room, but it also allows noise from outside, not to mention mosquitoes. This is particularly important should the company be working nights or splits. Changing sleep patterns from night to day can challenge even a healthy person.

The director is consulted on the production schedule. Shooting "nights" is often required as night: exterior cannot be duplicated on a stage. Switching the schedule from day to night photography is often done over a weekend so the call time for Monday starts at sundown. Unless one shoots an entire week at night, switching back to day photography can be complicated. An interesting option is to shoot splits, half days and half nights. Splits require a call time of noon and a wrap around midnight. This schedule is easier on the health of the cast and crew.

Film directing, the whole film business, is all consuming. Kurosawa once said that if you subtract cinema from Kurosawa you get nothing. This may be one reason why, after the failure of his first color film *Dodes-Ka-Den*, he took a hot bath and slashed himself with a razor 30 times. All work and no play make Sally a dull girl. Hollywood in particular is so caught up in the fast pace of doing business that wherever you find yourself, the subject of conversation is invariably the movies. "What film did you see last night? Did you finish your screenplay? Is that director seeing anyone else for the part? Why did she shoot her film digital? Who will be the next president of SAG? How did that Norwegian boy break the MPAA code?" etc.

It is not healthy to be involved in movies to the exclusion of everything else. Kazan makes it clear a director has to have all the answers, so time should be dedicated to the pursuit of interests other than the navel gazing associated with movies. It helps to have a hobby. Reading books is a good thing. Newspapers other than the trades are full of stories about the surrounding world. Museums can be enriching. Drawing, for example, is an activity that exercises the shifting of thought patterns from left to right brain. Tennis keeps one fit.

Sometimes travel or scheduling makes it difficult to maintain a family life during production. If feasible, blend family time into the production.

Robust health is so vital to a director that it earned its own chapter in this book. Good health influences the psychological considerations, which make up the subsequent chapters. A fit director controls the pace better, commands with more authority, and communicates with clarity. The entire focus of the project is funneled though the director, and the results will reflect that.

Psychology

The first five chapters of the book are practical in nature. A director has to have a screenplay, a cast, a crew, a budget and good health. Chapters 6 through 10 address the psychology of directing.

Craft is a blend of both the practical and the psychological. Craft is knowledge, how to do things. It has tangible qualities. It forms the bridge between the real and metaphysical world of film directing.

Craft is an accumulation of techniques and abilities specific to the profession that, when mastered, can be employed to manage a film set. One can direct a film knowing nothing of the craft. It helps, but the industry has many examples of writers insisting they be allowed to direct their screenplay as compensation, "carried" by a seasoned cast and crew.

Command is a key factor in the managing of a film set. Filmmaking is a series of problems to solve, and the buck stops with the director.

Pace refers to both the pace inherent in the screenplay and the swiftness with which the director directs.

Luck is an aspect of life over which a film director needs to maintain some control.

Chutzpah is boldness coupled with extreme self confidence. It is a trait film directors should exploit.

A Typical Day

- Cast and crew arrive on the set.
- Shot is blocked for the camera.
- Marks are placed on the floor for the actors and camera.
- The focus marks are set.
- The set is lit.
- Rehearsal occurs off set.
- Actors are dressed and made-up.
- A run-through is held for the actors and camera.
- Adjustments are made for the actors and camera.
- The scene is shot.
- The camera is moved for the next setup or sequence.

|◀◀   **6**   ▶▶|

Craft

The sound track says one thing, while the image says something else.
— Alfred Hitchcock

In his epic film *The Seven Samurai*, Akira Kurosawa employs a common and effective device to elucidate the story. Just before the samurai and the villagers collide with the savage brigands, one of the samurai sews a flag. An army, no matter how ragtag, does battle under a flag. The banner is comprised of six circles, representing the six samurai, a triangle and the Japanese character for farmers. Toshiro Mifune's character is the triangle, the seventh samurai, a farmer posing as a samurai. He represents the link between these two communities. In the same way, craft links the practical with the psychological aspects of filmmaking.

A director's craft is nurtured primarily through practice. The director's two best teachers are success and failure. Every director starts as a novice, asking questions, observing professionals and constantly learning. Directors who have not done their homework run the risk of having to hand over the project to a more seasoned cinematographer to carry the standard to the end of production.

The craft of directing can be broken down into ten categories: previsualization, working with actors, placing the camera, location sound recording, special effects, cheating, fix it post, short cuts, compression, and editing.

Previsualization

If the screenplay is a blueprint for a film, previsualization is the model built to show the client what the building will look like. The previsualization tools employed by the director include breakdowns, floor plans, storyboards, and a viewfinder.

Breakdowns

Directors keep a large notebook to record their thoughts on how to shoot the film. Camera moves, acting points, sound cues and equipment requirements are jotted down adjacent to the appropriate place in the screenplay. The number of extras, wardrobe specifications, notes for the art department, special camera equipment, etc., are included in these notes. Supplemental paperwork to the script at this juncture expands the notebook. Breakdowns are added based on what is required in the script, including the director's notes. Each item that is crucial to a specific shot is written down in the breakdown sheets. If it isn't on the sheet, then it won't be on the set.

Set Pieces

The director can look at the whole production schedule and identify the "set pieces" as a means of laying out the production board. A "set piece" is a big, important scene played out in one major location requiring several days of shooting. Set pieces become the cornerstones of the production schedule. Half-page scenes and drive-bys can be jockeyed around the shooting schedule, but set pieces need to be grounded in a particular location for a specific amount of time. Set pieces often require construction, rigging, special lighting, the works.

Floor Plans

Each scene requires a preliminary floor plan. On a sheet of paper, the four sides of the set or location are defined: a wall here, a window there, trees lining a walk, a pond, a house. These stationary set pieces are sketched onto the floor plan. Taking into account time of day and the arc of the sun, the director indicates the main camera positions.

The camera is marked as a "V" with the wider part of the letter pointed toward the action. A letter is placed next to the "V," thus identifying the camera position. A wide or establishing shot is indicated as shot "A," the two-shot "B" and so on. If camera position "B" is a tracking shot, the number "1" is placed next to the letter to indicate the beginning of the shot, or first position. The number "2" is placed at the end of the shot, or the final position. The notation B1 to B2 is drawn on the floor plan as a camera move. If the camera is to pause and then shift position more than once, additional numbers are added: B3 to B4 to B5, etc.

A legend is created on the floor plan to elaborate on any of the short-hand notations. A shot without notation usually means the camera will be placed at eye level. Shot A1 may be an overhead, or high-hat shot, so the notes make it clear to all parties what the director's intentions are for that particular camera position. Eventually the numbers will be prioritized and shape the initial schedule (interdepartmental communication is discussed in detail in Chapter 7: Command).

Storyboards

Once a floor plan is devised, some directors opt to storyboard the film. Storyboards are drawings of each shot planned for the movie. More crude than a comic book, and rarely colorized, storyboards delineate the previsualization of the film. An unprepared director walks onto a set and points toward the front door of the house and says to the crew, "The main character will exit the house and walk to his car there in the driveway." A frame is set up, the director rehearses the scene and decides to add a camera move, "Let's set up some track and walk with the character to his car." Tracks are now laid out, a new frame is rehearsed, and the director again has a change of mind, "Let's do the whole tracking shot in close-up." A new lens is popped onto the camera and the crew affects another run through. "I like the close up, but to include the background, lets move the track back ten feet." Ten feet later, the shot is ready for camera to roll.

The scenario above is not uncommon, even if the director had both floor plans and a storyboard indicating the tracking close-up shot. The script, floor plans and storyboards may be all thrown out the window once the company arrives on set. A whole new approach may strike the director as the scene is rehearsed. Magic may happen. A sensitive director is open to the alchemical process in making films.

But the time it takes to change camera positions three times is significant — perhaps an hour. An hour in a director's day is gold and should not be squandered. A storyboard explicitly laying out the shot would have told the director of photography exactly how to lay out the track and what lens to use, saving precious time.

Viewfinder

A viewfinder helps the director determine the exact size and focal length of a shot. On any set or location, the viewfinder is employed to see how a shot will look once the camera is placed. Utilizing a viewfinder is an efficient way to decide on an ideal position for the camera on set during the walk-through.

During pre-production the director begins to interpret the script by scouting locations, walk-throughs, and casting.

Scouting Locations

A location manager visits several locations as possible choices for principal photography, selecting the sites to show based on his or her own interpretation of the script as well as discussions with the director. The location manager factors in practical issues such as location fees, travel time, distance from the production office, dressing requirements, traffic, parking and about 2,607 other considerations.

At these initial locations, the location manager takes 360-degree panoramic photographs, mounts them on a board and shows them to the production staff. The director chooses one or two to visit. In this manner a location and one back-up are selected. When the location is locked, fees are negotiated, and as many practical considerations as possible are met, the director will take the key crew members for a walk-through.

Walk-Throughs

The walk-through consists of matching the floor plans and storyboards to the actual place in which they will shoot. Adjustments are then made to the drawings to reflect the real location. The director of photography notes the available light, practical lamps and power supplies, and suggests to the gaffer what lighting package to prepare for this particular location. The art director observes what needs to be replaced, protected or used for the scene, which in turn tells the set dresser what to prepare. The sound person checks out the locale for any sound problems, such as air conditioners or noisy traffic patterns.

Most cinematographers and sound recordists visit the set or location at different times of day to observe how shadows come and go with the arc of the sun and how traffic noise ebbs and flows. Although the sequence may be scheduled to be shot in the morning, changes may require shifting to an afternoon shoot. Experience helps to limit surprises, but alas, some are inevitable. Wittgenstein said: "When I came home I expected a surprise and there was no surprise for me, so, of course, I was surprised."

After the walk-through, the department heads sit down and indicate the lead-time they will require to prepare the set. The director of photography may want to pre-rig, or the art director may need the location or set for several days in order to dress it. All of this information is reflected in the constantly morphing production schedule.

Basic Steps to Arrive at a Shooting Plan
- Know the script.
- Know the theme.
- Know what each character wants in the story.
- Develop a history of the main characters.
- Break down each scene for dramatic beats.
- Determine a visual style for the story.
- Settle on pacing and tone.
- Create floor plans and storyboards.
- Make a shot list.

Cast

The director imagines the picture more clearly once an actor has been cast, because now there is a face to put on the character. The actor will be of a certain height, with a specific build and hairstyle. If any of the actor's physicality requires alteration, the art department has time to prepare. Wardrobe has to be bought and made (in doubles and triples), wigs, make-up tests, etc. All this takes time and must be completed prior to principal photography. If an actor is required in a scene to pick up a photograph of himself, his wife and daughter, that picture is taken, developed and framed weeks before it becomes set dressing in the film.

Working with Actors

Actors, in tandem with the director, create characters that propel the story. The actor and director base the arc of the character on the text of the screenplay. The expertise of the actor combined with the savvy of the director form a dance to the tune of the script. This choreography includes everything from finding the tempo of a specific beat, the handling of a key prop, the choice of wardrobe, the blocking in a scene, to the emotional balance between two characters.

As has been discussed, each shot is a single mosaic tile in the final picture. So, too, is an actor's performance composed of a series of beats, which, when assembled in continuity, create a credible character. Shaping these beats is the micro, the final performance the macro. The actor is involved each moment in performance, whether big or small, whereas the director is required to be both subjective and objective (see Chapter 7: Command). This is particularly important because the picture will more than likely be shot out of continuity. Therefore a director's key responsibility is guiding any performance to an emotional intensity consistent with the arc of the character as indicated by the screenplay.

Much of the staging of the scene may have been preplanned, through either storyboards, floor plans or walk-throughs with the actor and cinematographer. However, it is in the moment just prior to shooting a scene that everything gels. The lines, business, props, set dressing, camera movement, lighting and interaction between actors are primed for this shot. Though there has been an overall plan that organizes these elements for this moment, a director should take a deep breath and allow the moment to materialize organically.

To get to this juncture requires time. The actors go through their rehearsal paces at half speed, saving their energy for when the camera rolls. The blocking rehearsal maps out the action in a final pattern, which may or may not resemble the master plan. Things happen in this rehearsal that suddenly bring the scene to life. A director should be flexible and open to the creativity inherent in this eleventh-hour process.

After blocking the scene, the actors are sent back to make-up and hair for final touch ups. Meanwhile, the crew goes over and finalizes the lighting and camera plan. When both cast and crew are standing by, the director calls for a final dress rehearsal (see glossary). After this final rehearsal, when all is in readiness, the shot can be called.

It is a challenge to bring all the technical elements together in a creative instant. A director shouldn't rehearse too much on set for fear of stale performances. Nor should the director wing it, as the technical elements must be in complete harmony.

Actors must hit marks to be in focus and in the proper light. They must know their lines. Bits of business need to be executed at specified moments. Actors pick up their cues from other actors or at a prearranged signal. While performing these technical duties, actors realize a performance. And all the above must be repeated exactly for each different camera angle.

There are many styles and schools of acting. The director has to discern which methods work best for which actors. A Stanislavski-trained actor may take several takes to get into character. An improv-trained actor may be most fresh on the first and second takes, thus motivating the director to shoot multiple cameras. An actor dependant on extreme make-up works from the tip of his or her fake nose toward the center of the character, which may take time, while other actors find their truest moments through props and set dressing. Rehearsals are usually played at half-speed, a take at full speed. The director's challenge is to unite the actor's pacing and acting styles within the scene.

Magic can occur just before the director calls for "action" and between the end of the scene and when the director calls "cut." Since the actor will stay in character until the director says "action" or "cut," behavior may slip out and onto the film or tape during these unscripted moments. In the editing room, the director often looks for moments of action, eye and/or facial movements that intensify a scene.

A scene is shot or covered from several angles. Even if the plan is for the scene to be photographed in a single take, inserts and pick-ups should be taken for safety in the editing room. In a long take, a director may like 75 percent of the shot but feel that some portion of it unusable. This is often the case if an actor nails a scene but blows the last line. Rather than reshoot the entire shot, the director may call for a pick-up on the tag of the sequence, just to cover the last line. In this manner, the director can cut from the usable material to the pick-up while maintaining emotional continuity.

Actors focus their eyes on the actors with whom they are performing a scene. Alone, an actor may choose an object upon which to concentrate. When bouncing the camera from one set up to the next, it is the responsibility of the camera operator, script supervisor and director to keep track of the direction in which the actor is looking. This is referred to as the actor's eye line. In a two-character scene, the actor looks left to right. When the camera turns around to shoot the lines and reactions of the other actor, he or she must be looking right to left. When cutting from one actor to the other, the perception on the part of the audience will be that the characters are speaking to one another.

If an actor has been dismissed for the day, or is not available to stand by the camera to give the actor someone to look at, the director often takes that position. If there is no room next to the camera for the other actor or the director to stand, the assistant cameraman will place a small flag or brightly colored piece of tape for the actor to look at. In this way, the actor's eye line will be focused on the proper spot or direction. The tape or focus spot for the actor may be directly at the edge of the lens. Actors and camera operators need to be mindful the eyes do not cross the center of the lens. Actors can look at all parts of the periphery of the lens, but when their eyes look directly down the barrel of the lens, the fourth wall is broken.

In the theater, on a proscenium stage, there exist three walls: the back and two sides. The fourth wall is the invisible one between the audience and the stage. When the curtain falls, it makes this fourth wall a solid. The invisible, or fourth, wall makes the audience feel it is peeking in upon an unfolding drama. Even in an inner monologue soliloquy, an actor speaks out directly to the audience, but does not make eye contact with them. The actor speaks much like the interior dialogues in a novel. So, too, in film an audience comes to a theater, takes a seat, and watches the drama unfold on the silver screen. The actors on the screen rarely make eye contact with the audience. If they did, it would make the audience uncomfortable, as if the magic and mystery were suddenly dispelled.

If an actor or an extra in a scene looks even for an instant at the lens, the effect is startling to the viewer. Avoid it at all cost. The exception is in a comedy. There are moments when an actor, during a slow burn (see glossary), or to include the audience in a joke, makes a point of looking at the lens. An example of this kind of "nudge, nudge, get it?" moment occurs is when Peter Boyle, as Frankenstein's monster in Mel Brooks' film *Young Frankenstein*, sits with the little gypsy girl at the edge of the lake. They are tearing petals off a flower. When the little girl sees the last petal is gone, she looks up and asks the monster, "Oh, what shall we throw in the water now?" Peter Boyle reacts by looking at us, the audience, and grins. Without actually seeing it, it is clear what, or in this case who, will be tossed into the water next.

A director also needs to be aware of possible disturbances in the actor's sight line. If a group of crew members is standing behind the camera are in the eye line of the actor, it may prove distracting. Keeping the actor's eye line clear assists the actor's concentration.

During the actual shooting, the only crew members authorized to speak to an actor besides the director are the script supervisor and the director of photography. Hair and make-up artists stand by for quick touch-ups. The director creates an amiable atmosphere during the intense period of shooting. He is the calm at the eye of the storm, allowing the work of shaping a character and a scene to progress without interference.

The script supervisor maintains continuity so that all material sent to the editing room will cut together without noticeable jumps or mistakes. Let's say an actor points to one character in a wide shot, but in the medium shot mistakenly points to another character. The two shots will not cut. This is when the script supervisor reminds the actor where to point. Eye lines, what hand which prop was in, matching wardrobe and a myriad of other things from one camera angle to the next require extraordinary scrutiny on the part of the script supervisor (also called *continuity*).

Script supervisors' notes include the following:
- Brief description of what happened during the take
- At what point in a scene an actor does what
- Length of each shot (timed with a stopwatch)
- Lens used
- Director's comments
- DP's comments

The cinematographer has access to the actor in technical matters only. The director of photography wants to have the light fall just right on an actor. Actors must hit, or stop at, certain marks taped to the floor. Therefore, a director of photography can "direct" actors to ensure they are photographed correctly. The director is the only person on set who can shout "cut" to stop the camera from rolling. In extreme circumstances, however, when an actor is badly out of focus, or the boom dips deep into the frame, the cinematographer (or operator) can signal to cut.

Placing the Camera

The camera is the director's eye, and since film is visual storytelling, the camera is the director's most important tool. If the sound system in a theater were to cease functioning, and the audience had no choice but to continue to watch the film, the story should still be clear. Dialogue, sound effects and music are vital to a film, but the image is dominant.

The screenplay contributes the bulk of information that directors require to formulate a shooting plan. Broad strokes are established by the genre of the story. A comedy is usually bright and colorful, whereas a horror film is dark and atmospheric. A script might scream out to be shot in black and white, sepia tones or pastels. Camera placement and moves are dictated by genre. Comedy can hold a static frame as the actors perform routines, while the conventions of a horror film prescribe low-angle POV tracking shots to scare the audience into thinking "someone or something is coming to get me!"

But if the screenplay is a blueprint, the director produces ideas that visualize the drama. Directors examine the sequence and determine how to shoot it. They consider everything, from the important (how does this sequence fit into the whole?) to the trivial (should the actor tap his watch to see if it is working or just read the time?). Whatever the director decides, the camera will play an important part in that judgment.

Besides normal shots, directors also consider where to place the sound recording devices so they do not enter the frame. Special on-set effects like fire and stunts, as well as the coordination of CGI photography that will take place after principle photography, affect how and where to place the camera or cameras. There are dozens of short cuts or "cheats" a director can employ to ensure the camera is telling the story in the time allotted to the production company.

Major choices are made in pre-production: the look of the film, aspect ratio, and the choice of stock, lens selection, and variety of movement. The shot selection process is the same, no matter how big or from what angle the image is taken. The basic unit of a film, the shot is to the whole as the tile is to the mosaic. As you cut from one scene to the next, make sure to imbue each shot with an emotional arc, information, composition, motivation and continuity. Only a shot containing these elements is worth sending on to the editing room. Underdeveloped shots, those that contain no information or motivation or neglect continuity, are more often than not eliminated.

A gestalt is a pattern of elements so unified it's impossible to see its constituents. That's the way a good film appears — so unified that each shot fits in seamlessly with the design of the overall picture. You achieve this by choosing a lens, an angle and a camera position to get a shot that can be low, high, close, distant, soft, hard, static, and/or moving. Then frame-by-frame, you piece together the arc of the whole story.

Shooting Ratio

An early budget question is how much film stock to purchase. This is the paper onto which directors write their story. Too much is a waste (film is nonrefundable), and too little could jeopardize the integrity of the project, forcing the editor to make difficult and/or awkward cuts. When shooting in 16 mm or 35 mm, the director of photography orders all stock from one batch. Because rolls have consecutive serial numbers, this guarantees consistent picture quality and control. Film that is not from sequential batches could be of slightly different grain size and color quality. Shooting on tape is less critical, and the cost is so minuscule that too much tape is never a problem.

The average amount used on a feature film is about 150,000 feet, although one can be shot on as little as 30,000 feet and as much as a million. The average length of a roll of 35 mm film is 1,000 feet. Therefore, every additional 1,000 feet you shoot adds a number to the shooting ratio. If a feature exposes 150,000 feet of film, the shooting ratio is 15:1. That means that for every foot used in the final print, 14 were left out. It is said John Ford shot *Grapes of Wrath* on 30,000 feet of film. This means he shot an astoundingly low 3:1 ratio. It also means he knew exactly what he wanted out of each camera position. Some directors keep themselves to a low ratio. For instance Buñuel said he never used more than 20,000 meters (approximately 66,600 feet) of celluloid. It's all in the planning.

Film stock of 150,000 feet to 200,000 feet is an average for a film. Anything over 250,000 feet is a lot. Under 50,000 is tight. In filmmaking the two things upon which a director never concedes are the amount of stock and the number of PAs. One must always have ample stock. At no point in the making of a motion picture should the production manager have to go to the director and say they cannot continue shooting because the company has run out of stock. A picture can have many slow downs for any number of reasons. Stock should not be one of them. Directors shooting digital need not be concerned about stock. As for having enough PAs, so many people want to work in the movies that labor is not a problem, and when a picture needs people to work the traffic or move crowds around the frame, a shortage of PAs should not be a factor.

Coverage

The first question a director asks upon arriving on set is how to cover the sequence scheduled for that day. Coverage (and its partner, continuity) refers to the different angles from which a particular scene is shot. For instance, one can shoot two lovers kissing from several angles. Ensure choices in the editing room.

Once in the editing room, with a range of angles from which to choose, a sequence can cut together seamlessly to get the desired result. Scenes can be covered in many ways, from a single take (no edits) to multiple set-ups. The director maps out the plan for the shots and then, with the director of photography, script supervisor and assistant director, determines the order in which to shoot them.

Continuity ensures that all the elements from one shot match in every way the elements in the shot that follows. Props, wardrobe, hair, make-up and acting are the departments that get close scrutiny by the script supervisor, director and cinematographer. If an actress holds a book in her right hand during a sequence, every shot must show the book in the correct hand. If the actress changes it to the left hand halfway through the scene, all shots must match the correct progression of the book from one hand to the next. In another instance, we see a character walk into a building wearing a red shirt. Several days later the scene is shot in which the character exits the same building. It is imperative that actor be wearing the same shirt. In this same example, should the character open the door to exit the building in a great huff, when the reverse shot is executed from the exterior, the energy level must match that of the character leaving the building, still in a huff. Should the character saunter out of the building, the cut from interior to exterior, which takes place in an instant, may jar the audience. Maintaining continuity is everyone's job. Continuity errors do occur, and often go unnoticed by the audience. But don't count on it. It's similar to making a bad grammatical error in a beautiful piece of writing. It takes the focus away from what is important.

180° Rule

One of the more confusing areas of coverage has to do with the 180° rule. Although it is not inviolable (many directors have disregarded this rule), cutting from one character speaking to another character can look odd if the rule is not followed. The eye-line, or where a character is looking, relates to screen direction. Viewers must be able to follow the eye-line from the character's eyes to what the character sees. The camera operator needs to be sure of the match so that the cut will work in the editing room. If the director never crosses the 180° line, a character will always appear to be looking at the person to whom he is speaking.

Shots

Shots are either static (the camera remains stationary) or in movement, or a combination of the two. In the same way, actors may be stationary or in motion, or a combination of the two. The interaction between camera and actor is referred to as *choreography*.

The most common types of shots used are the master, mini-master, two shot, over the shoulder, and close up. These may be shot static on a tripod or mounted on a dolly, jib arm, crane or hand held for movement.

The master shot is popular because it takes in all the action of the scene. Once a master is in the can, the coverage must match the master. This helps to guide the remaining plan. To break up a big or long scene, a director might select to shoot several mini-masters.

When two characters are in a scene, the director employs a two shot to hold them both on the screen. The director can still keep both characters in a scene but favor the back or ¾ profile of one of the characters in an over-the-shoulder shot. The frame features the character looking toward the camera, but the dynamic of having both characters on screen remains.

The size of shot is also an important consideration in a shooting sequence. Directors can choose between the following:

- extreme long shot (XLS)
- long shot (LS)
- medium long shot (MLS)
- medium shot (MS)
- medium close-up (MCU — also referred to as a bust shot)
- close-up (CU)
- extreme close-up (XCU)

The director indicates to the director of photography and actors a specific frame size by using their hands to show the size of the shot. Showing one hand slightly over the head, and the other at chest level means a bust shot. When staging actors, directors also need to identify how many characters are in a shot. A two shot means two actors, a three shot has three actors, etc. The director also selects shots such as over-the-shoulder (OTS) to maintain the tension and relationship within the frame of two characters yet seeing the face of only one.

To isolate one of the characters, the director shoots a single or close-up. The single takes in much of the actor's torso and head, whereas the close-up features the face. When the director wants to accent the eyes or another part of the face, then an extreme close-up (XCU) is used.

Alfred Hitchcock used the camera to explore subtext: "The sound track says one thing, while the image says something else. That's a fundamental of film directing. Isn't it exactly the way it is in real life? People don't always express their inner thoughts to one another; a conversation may be quite trivial, but often the eyes will reveal what a person thinks or feels."

Two additional common shots are establishing and insert. An establishing shot is used when a director wants the audience to know where it is to have a reference point. Two characters sitting on a park bench could be anywhere in the world. A wide, establishing shot of the Eiffel Tower tells the audience that they are in Paris. The next shot, a two shot of our main characters on a bench, makes the geography of the scene clear.

An insert is a close shot of something the director wants the audience or a character to see. The hand of the man on the bench holds a wedding ring. The girl clutches a plane ticket to Kabul. These close-ups help tell the story.

Each shot has an angle. For the most part, directors shoot at eye level. However, great effect can come from a low-angle, high-angle, or tilted (canted or dutch) shot. The director John Huston once said, "It would be very hard to make someone, even a comedian, amusing or funny by shooting up at them. I don't say this couldn't be done, but I think it probably comes from our memories as children — from those that are bigger, wiser, stronger, nobler. We look up — same as you do with sculpture, monumental sculpture. Would you look down at your superior, or even God Almighty?"

Lens

- ECU — extreme close-up (eyes and nose)
- CU — close-up (complete face)
- MS — medium shot (torso)
- WS — wide shot (full body)
- LS — long shot (full body in landscape)
- XLS — extreme long shot (small body in vista)

Lenses

Each shot is taken with a particular lens. These range from wide angle (10mm) to normal (35 mm/50 mm) to long (75 mm to 200 mm). Extreme lenses, employed for specific dramatic effect, include fish eye (5.7 mm) and very long (500 mm and longer). A lens can keep the subject in the frame sharp, or in focus, depending on the amount of light striking the lens, the focal length of the lens, and the depth of field. A wide-angle lens, for example, lets in a lot of light, so most objects in the frame are always in focus. A longer lens, in a dimly lit set-up, may focus on the actor while everything else in the foreground and background is blurred, or out of focus. This latter example can make for a visually striking effect that implies to an audience that the character is in a private world. The image of isolation can also be accomplished by shooting a character in an extremely wide long shot from a high angle set against a barren landscape. The combination of lens, proximity to the subject, depth of field and angle of the camera makes for hundreds of options available to the director to visualize the story.

Besides these basic shots, directors come to rely on other shots that have specific relevance related to the story. These include the reveal, point-of-view, and reaction shots.

The audience sees only the rectangular image on the screen. Whatever is to the left or right, above or below the frame is said to be "off screen." If the camera dollies, zooms, tilts or pans to show us what we cannot see, this is a "reveal." It is excellent visual storytelling because the shot builds tension as the camera moves to inform the audience of something they may be curious to learn about. The camera settles, and something is revealed, satisfying the audience.

A powerful example of the reveal is seen in Alfred Hitchcock's film *Psycho*. Immediately after the violent death of the main character in the shower, the camera tracks ever so slowly from her open eye, past the bathroom door, into the bedroom, over to the end table, and settles on a folded newspaper. This key prop hides the $40,000 that Janet Leigh's character has embezzled. The shock of the stabbing in the shower has added emotional value: the main character has been killed and the film is only half over. This is unusual in a film and one of the great story twists in cinema. All the while processing this information — the violent murder, the violation of the privacy of a shower, the elimination of the main character — when the camera settles on the newspaper the audience realizes for the first time that this is no longer a story of a crime of greed, but a crime of passion. That one shot, that reveal, that seemingly innocuous shot of the newspaper, packs quite a wallop.

When the camera becomes the character, it is called a point-of-view shot. A character looks off camera, shouts, "Hey you!" and the cut is made to what the character sees. We see the character walking cautiously down an alley. The cut is made to the character's point of view, hand held, so it has a bit of movement, as a person walking would have and looking ahead. Add some tense music, and the audience immediately wants to know who or what is at the end of the alley.

One of the more common and important shots in film grammar is the reaction shot. When two or more characters are in a scene, the director has the choice of shooting the character that is speaking and/or the character listening. In most cases, all the lines from one character are shot from a particular angle, and the camera is then reversed to shoot the other character's lines. Included in the shooting is the period when the characters say nothing. This is the reaction shot. The editor then has the option of using either the on-screen dialogue or the reaction shot of the listening. Once the characters have been established, the value of the reaction shot is that the audience hears the dialogue at the same time they see the reaction of the person listening. We, as an audience, can then share both the character's reaction to the dialogue as well as our own.

Choreography

Once frame selections are made, the director has the option to keep the camera static or in motion. A static camera presents a stage, or proscenium, in which the drama unfolds. In the early days of cinema, cameras were so heavy and bulky, the static shot was the director's sole option. Cinema was born out of a still camera, and the static camera still has value today.

Once cameras were put on tracks, and became lighter and smaller, directors found that a moving frame created a tremendous amount of energy. This freedom of movement added an element to cinematic expression that compounded the tension within the shot.

Directors can move the actors in the frame, move the frame around the actors, or a combination of the two. Camera movement includes pans, tilts, zooms, dolly, crane and hand held. The movement may be short or long, fast or slow. The speed may be altered in any manner within the shot.

Creating Camera Movement

- Pan
- Tilt
- Pan/tilt combination
- Zoom (cheap dolly)
- Dolly (with or without tracks)
- Trucking shot
- Hand-held camera work
- Crane
- Steadicam(r)
- Car, helicopter, boat (traveling shots)

Moving the actors within the camera choreography is the blocking. As with lighting, the movement of the camera should be purposeful. A flashy camera may overshadow a subtle film. In a busy restaurant the director can have the camera follow a waiter holding a tray of food through the room and then settle on the main characters.

Consider the following when you compose a shot:

- Camera placement
- Composition of shot
- Use of color or black and white

- Type of shot
- Size of shot
- Camera movement
- Shot perspectives
- Coverage
- Continuity
- Specialty shots
- Lighting
- Editing

Composition, besides having aesthetic value, is important because it allows the director to direct the audience's eye to that part of the shot deemed most important to tell the story. If the entire frame were busy with action in a long shot, it would say, "Everyone is bustling about." But if the director wants the audience to focus on an argument at the lower right-hand corner of the frame, he or she can compose the shot in such as way as to have the audience's eye drawn to that section of the frame. This can be achieved through blocking, lighting, camera movement and sound.

To illustrate: the blocking of the background extras could be staged so they move more slowly than the animated actors engaged in the argument. The lighting could be dominant in the portion of the frame where the dispute is taking place. The camera could dolly in the direction of the arguing characters. The sound of their heated discussion could be emphasized over the ambient sounds associated with everything else in the frame.

Depth is part of the illusion to be found on a flat, two-dimensional screen. Directors take advantage not only of the composition within the frame, but also of the planes in the frame — foreground, middle and background. Shooting a sequence with the branch of a tree covering the upper right part of the frame forces the audience to look beyond the tree, thus creating the illusion of depth on the screen. Action can be staged on all three planes, layering the scene with complex imagery. The director can also call attention to a specific part of the frame by racking the focus from background, to middle ground, to foreground.

Architecture, size, relationship and negative space are tools that the director and cinematographer can use to create a dynamic frame. In designing *Psycho*, Hitchcock consciously juxtaposed Norman Bates' tall Gothic house with the low, modern hotel, "That's our composition, a vertical block and a horizontal block."

Besides what an audience sees on screen, the director should pay attention to what is happening off screen. The four sides of the frame are constantly shifting if the camera is moving. Therefore, new information is being revealed. Curious about this new information, an audience is eager to be surprised. Off-screen sounds, illustrating off-screen action, make an audience curious to know what else is going on. Remember, the reveal is one of the more dynamic uses of cinematic language.

An unmotivated camera movement can be jarring. There is nothing wrong with a fixed lens if it is the right choice to tell that part of the story.

Motivate the Camera

- To follow the movement of a character
- To allow a vehicle to motivate a camera move down a street
- To establish a landscape or scene geography
- To move in to a character to intensify our relationship with a character or object
- To move away from someone or something to see it more objectively
- To move to reveal important information
- To move to reframe or accommodate a rearrangement of characters
- To move the camera up or down for dramatic purposes

Lighting

A black screen tells us that the characters themselves are in darkness. Illuminate one small part of the scene and the audience's eye is drawn to it. Light the entire scene, but concentrate more light on a specific character and the audience's eye is drawn to that character. Cinematography is often referred to as "painting with light."

Film examples and stills assist the director and director of photography in finding a style and look for the film. Storyboards help even more by previsualizing the look of each shot. The essence of the lighting plan is dictated by location and time of day. A sauna in Greenland during the summer is a very different look than a jungle at dusk. Sunrise tends toward blue light, whereas a sunset glows with yellow and orange. High noon has a harsher light than dusk, while cloudy days have an even light compared to the harsh shadows on a cloudless desert. The language of film lighting requires discussions and decisions about the following:

SOURCE

Unless the sequence is intentionally unnatural, as in a dream scene, light sources are based on the logic of the location and time of day. Any setting, exterior or interior, is lit to duplicate reality. Within this framework, cinematographers have some leeway, or artistic license, to enhance the scene artificially while still sticking to the basic plan of authenticity. During the day, a room with a big window will use the sun as the main source of light. The main light always comes from this direction. At night, practical lamps will illuminate a pool hall just above the pool tables.

KEY

The director of photography considers the source and uses it as the key or brightest light. During the day, in most cases, the sun is the source light. During the night, lamps over the pool tables will light the characters.

HARD OR SOFT

Light has qualities such as hard (harsh) or soft (diffused). The mood of a scene is greatly affected by the quality of light. For example, comedies use bright lights, while horror films tend to use shadows and shafts of light for effect.

NATUÏRAL OR ARTIFICIAL

Cinematographers measure light with a light meter. The stock in the camera is sensitive to specific kinds of light. Some stock is made to be shot outdoors (daylight), while others are used exclusively for interiors (tungsten). The color in the stock is affected differently when shooting with the sun as a source as opposed to using tungsten lamps. While there are filters and special tricks to manipulate the temperature of the stock, a director of photography is constantly balancing the equation of the stock + light + subject + mood + intent.

Lighting

- How will the scene be lit?
- Where is the light source?
- Where will your source light come from?
- If the location has windows, how long will the set receive direct sunlight?

- Is there ample space to place the lights in the location?
- Can you prerig or rough in any lights before the day of the shoot?
- Can you put spreaders on the ceiling without damaging the walls?
- Will you need to provide a fan to cool the room?
- For an exterior, will the sun provide adequate light for proper exposure, or will you have to supplement the sunlight? Will you need silks to even out the light?

Instruments on set that are part of the dressing are termed *practicals*. Let's imagine a character enters a room during the day where the sun streaming in through the window is the light source. If he or she turns a lamp (practical) on in the shot, it must be bright enough to look realistic. Gaffers (electricians) work with set dressers to rewire and place high intensity bulbs in practical lamps. This is so they will be bright enough to register on the film stock temperature balanced to match the source light.

SHADOWS, SILHOUETTES, HIGHLIGHTS AND EDGES

Once the basic lighting plan is roughed in, the cinematographer adds details to the scene with the lights. For example, the shadows in the scene can be milky or deep black. Characters can be lit so they blend in with the background or backlit so an edge of light makes them stand out from the background. Pin spots can highlight the eyes, the hair, a key prop or a puddle of water. A flag or cookie (see glossary) can be placed so as to block some of the light, which creates an interesting shadow or dappled effect.

EXTERIORS

The sun is the predominant source of light in exterior shooting. Though cinematographers prefer a cloudy day for the diffused light that it offers, a crew can work in the bright sun without any lights at all. If the sun is too harsh, grips can set up large white silks that hover over the actors for tight shooting. The even light that comes through the silk is consistent. As in every department, lighting needs to follow the logic of continuity rules. Cutting from a brightly lit face to a dark face can be jarring to the viewer.

Because the light from the sun is bright shining down on actors, gaffers provide bounce boards or shiny boards that, when placed correctly, bounce the sunlight back up into the faces of the actors. This allows the camera to see faces without blowing out (overexposing) the background. When the day is too dark, lights can be brought on set to fill in and create highlights. They are powered by a portable generator placed many feet away to avoid the noise made by the generator. These instruments can fill in and create highlights when the day is too dark. Directors and their crews are constantly "chasing the sun" during exterior shoots. Sunset often determines the end of the workday for many of the crew since exposure levels drop until there is not enough light to shoot a scene.

INTERIORS

Shooting in a practical location or on a sound stage requires a lot of light. Dozens of instruments, hundreds of feet of cable, multiple "C" stands (see glossary) and a mountain of gels, scrims and flags are used. The cinematographer, starting with the source, sets up the larger instruments that will generate the majority of the light. Then, little by little, the smaller instruments, flags to cut the big lights, gels and scrims (if necessary), are set up, and the scene is ready for photography.

One of the advantages of shooting interiors is the control over light. The arc of the sun affects exteriors, as do clouds, wind and weather. Interior light is fixed. A director can shoot an interior scene during the day or night. Even on a practical location, if the scene is set at night, but it is in fact daytime, the grips can set up a frame outside each door and window. Then they cover the frame with light-proof black velour, position tungsten-balanced lights with blue gels inside the tent, and it can be nighttime all day long.

COLOR

Most films are shot in color. Black-and-white films are a thing of the past, though occasionally contemporary filmmakers insist the story they plan to shoot needs to be shot in black and white. Color is an integral part of the style determined by the director, cinematographer and art director. Colors and patterns form the distinctive quality specific to each film.

ON SET

The camera operator, eye glued to the eyepiece, is the only one who sees the frame during a take. The operator is responsible for proper framing and for monitoring focus. The focus puller, who sits next to the operator, maintains focus by delicately dialing the focal ring on the lens. If, during the course of a take, the focus puller makes a mistake, the operator can inform the script supervisor following the take that all or parts of the shot were soft. If the error is significant, the operator can either stop the take or inform the director, immediately after "cut" is yelled, that the take is unusable. When a take is completed and the operator makes no comment to either the director or the script supervisor, it is assumed that everything is in focus.

Pulling focus takes years of practice. In the course of a tracking shot, a focus puller may have to rack the lens any number of times to keep the principal actor or actors in sharp focus. The focus puller places tape on the floor with corresponding numbers to the tape on the lens. As the actor moves from position number one to position two, the focus puller inches the lens ring to match each station.

The operator is also responsible for the frame line separating the action from the microphone boom. A boom dipping into the frame has ruined many a shot. Most boom operators have a knack for staying out of the frame yet keeping the boom close to the actors' lips. This is called *headroom*. Directors like to record quality sound during principal photography but not at the expense of retakes necessitated by a dipping boom.

A director can see the frame along with the operator with the aid of video-tap; otherwise they are available for first-time viewing only at dailies the following day. Many companies employ video-tap, also called video-assist, during filming. This is a television monitor that displays what the camera is recording. This tool has both value and drawbacks.

Video-tap is a tool like any other piece of equipment on set. Used properly, it is an asset to the production. It can also become a crutch and a trap. Video-assist is particularly valuable when attached to a recorder and played back for the director when he or she is also acting. The drawbacks of video-assist include the cost, plus the size and poor quality of the image. It can be deceptive to watch the video tap and judge the film as one in the same. Film picks up much more nuance and inflection than the video monitor. The image is compromised even further when it is screened during editing on the monitor of a nonlinear editing system.

A further shortcoming of video-tap is that everyone stands around the monitor as if they are watching television. It invites the producers, agents, managers, actors and department heads to become instant critics, judging every shot and making suggestions to the director. Too many cooks spoil the broth. In addition, the image is so small it fails to deliver the impact of the big screen experience. The glory of cinema is its ability to fill the big-screen, to encourage the viewer to study and appreciate the multiple layers embedded in the frame.

Army Archerd wrote in his *Daily Variety* column (July 30, 2002) that when Scorsese visited Lucas recently at Skywalker to see his demonstration of new technology, they posed for a picture together. "Army labeled us 'The Old' and 'The New,'" laughed Scorsese, who prefers to capture his actors' emotions on film cameras rather than digital. "Even when I am looking at the video monitor on the set," he admits, "I often have to go on the set to see the emotion on the actor's face which the film cameras will capture."

The film industry has adapted to several technological advancements over the years: sound, color, television, and now digital imagery. Some say 3D is the next frontier. The principles of cinema have pretty much remained constant: one image follows another to tell a compelling story that has an emotional effect on an audience. But the tools have changed, and will continue to do so. A director must be aware and familiar with any and all technological advancements in the industry. The documentary *Vision of Light* is a marvelous examination of how cameramen have re-tooled cameras over the years to accommodate the director's vision. Films are still shot on 35mm film, but eventually it will be replaced by digital imagery.

The shift to digital will bring down costs, and allow for more flexibility in creating an image. A flood of digital information will flow smoothly from camera to editing station to print to projection. Questions about copyright, archiving and quality will be addressed during the evolution from film to digital. Currently there are two digital modifications in the film industry, in post-production (99 percent of all films are cut on nonlinear digital systems such as Avid or Final Cut Pro) and in visual (CGI) effects.

Location Sound Recording

It is the goal of both the director and the sound recordist to bring good quality location sound to the editing room. On set there is a dance between the camera frame line and the boom pole. The microphones must be close enough to pick up the sounds that come from the actor, especially their text, but far enough from the frame line as to not "dip into the frame."

Sound

- Is the location quiet?
- Is there an abnormal amount of traffic outside?
- Can you use sound blankets to dull the traffic noise?
- Is the outside noise the same all day long?
- Do the neighbors have a noisy dog or child that must be quieted?
- Can existing sounds, such as refrigerators or air conditioning units, be silenced during shooting?
- Can the shots be planned so that the microphones point away from the windows?
- Are there plans for construction nearby during the shooting period?

The sound mixer will find time during rehearsals to spot the most efficient way to record sound for the shot. It might be done with a boom, a radio microphone, a planted microphone or a combination of the three.

A production sound mixer needs to consider:

- How large is the space?
- What are the acoustics of the space? (Hard surfaces reflect sound.)
- Can a loud refrigerator or air conditioning system be shut down?
- Can neighbors be controlled?
- Are key windows right above traffic noise?
- If the location is near an airport, what are the air traffic patterns?
- Will sound blankets solve the noise problems?
- What time of day will the shooting occur, and how is the local traffic at that time?

The sounds on a location will forever be part of the production track. This is why sound stages are called sound stages; there is total control of the sound. On location the sound mixer will ask that air conditioners, refrigerators, fans and any electronic or "humming" equipment be silenced during a take. The sound recordist has less control over traffic, overhead planes or barking dogs. The director will wait as long as possible for the setting to be as quiet as possible. If at a certain point, it becomes apparent that sounds cannot be controlled, the director will shoot despite the sound issues.

The director should be aware that disturbing sounds not only may dirty the track but may also distract the actors.

Special Effects

Special effects play an important part in many films. Whether it is the marauding dinosaurs in *Jurassic Park*, the dazzling slow-motion fight sequences in *The Matrix*, or just lighting a fire in a fireplace, experts are called in to produce the desired illusion. Special effects are either real-time effects produced on set (such as fire or prosthetic make-up) or manipulated images, created entirely in post-production. In both cases how and where the camera is placed needs to be coordinated with a team of technicians.

On-set effects require a special effects supervisor and assistants. Sometimes special effects include a stunt, in which case the special effects supervisor and the stunt coordinator collaborate on the shot. Special effects make-up, if simple enough, can be applied by the company make-up artist. Complicated make-up and prosthetic designs are handled by a separate company contracted for this one aspect of the film.

Elaborate live action shots, such as tank and miniature photography, are executed by a second unit team so as not to take up the time of the first unit. Complicated blue- or green-screen shots often employ the efforts of both the first and second unit. When Steven Spielberg was making *Jurassic Park*, Dennis Muren, head of special effects at George Lucas' visual effects company, ILM (Industrial Light and Magic), was given the task of animating the dinosaurs. The director asked that the dinosaurs move freely around the characters. This had never been done before. Usually effect shots place the mythical creatures behind or in front of the actors, who are standing in front of a giant blue screen and pretend to look up at monsters and reptiles that are not there. Interaction was impossible. Until Dennis Muren, working with his Industrial Light and Magic software team over the course of a year, devised a program that complied with the directors' request. Muren was quoted after the film as saying that from here on out, directors no longer have to compromise their vision.

Post-production effects, also called optical and/or digital effects, have become big business. Special effect companies, called houses, have sprung up in many cities to service the film and television communities. The special effect houses specialize in enhancing and creating images that either cannot be created on set or must be created on a computer, which enhances the production value of a shot for a fraction of what it would cost in principal photography. A green-screen shot, for example, is executed first on set with the principal actors with the backgrounds added later in post-production.

Cheating

A wonderful blend of craft and psychology is found in the uniquely film-centric definition for "cheating." Elsewhere the word has negative connotations. One thinks of Air Force cadets getting their hands on exam papers or CPAs with elaborate schemes to bilk their clients. But filmmaking embraces and even exalts the term as it applies to the filmmaking process.

If an actor of small stature has an intimate dialogue scene with a tall actress, the director will ask the grips to "fly in" a half apple box upon which the actor can stand. This is "cheating" so that one can get a good angle on the two shot and over-the-shoulder coverage. If the light enters a room through a window, the cinematographer may ask the actor to "cheat" his or her position to take better advantage of the angle of the light. The adjustment is not a move — it has to match the other coverage — but merely a slight alteration to accommodate the frame. Anything within the frame can be "cheated": wardrobe, hair, props, set dressing, lights, and actors.

Cheating has spawned other film-centric terms such as *fix it post*, *short cuts*, and *compression*.

Fix It Post

Shots are created in production or in post-production. Many films are created entirely during production with no reliance on images generated in post-production. Other films require additional photography in post-production to enhance or create shots.

Because the pressure to make the pages is so great during the shooting period, directors are prone to consider "fixing it in post." While many aspects of the filmmaking process can indeed be fixed (negative scratches, muddy sound, optically enhanced digital imagery), it is important that the director shoot as much principal photography as possible during production.

One problem with "fixing it in post" is that funds may not be available. Films are expensive and unpredictable. A director may discover that money allotted for post-production expenses, such as score, ADR, miniatures and opticals, has been compromised. Using budgeted money from post-production to ensure making it through principle photography is known as "robbing Peter to pay Paul."

There is a great deal to be said for theatrical versus optical photography. For one thing, there is no generation loss on the stock. And while magical images can be created in the digital realm, they often come at a steep price. A big effects movie is by its very nature an expensive endeavor. Each shot that employs green screen, digital matte work or even color correction, is expensive. Working on a tight budget, one would be wise to shoot a sequence during principal photography, if at all possible, rather than post-production.

The pre-production period is invaluable to a director. A plan is devised that will determine when and how each shot will be taken all through the many weeks of principle photography. During brainstorming sessions with key crew members, the approach to each sequence is discussed and an artistically yet fiscally responsible solution is arrived at. The solution to a difficult shot or sequence can easily be solved with buckets of money. With thoughtful deliberations, however, an inexpensive solution may be found that fulfills the director's vision.

Such was the case in a sequence from the live-action musical film *Sleeping Beauty* directed by the author. In this 35mm film, a scene called for eight fairies to attend a banquet dinner where they would bestow their gifts on the King and Queen's newborn daughter.

The director's image of fairies should try to match that of the audience. To give the actresses an ethereal presence, we chose slow-motion photography, mechanical wings, colorful costumes and lustrous lighting. For the dance sequence during which they bestow their gifts, we planned to have them be the only ones in frame, allowing us to film at 96fps. But there was one shot, a wide angle of the entire banquet room that called for the fairies to be in the same frame as the King, Queen and their 50 guests.

During pre-production, we dedicated hours of deliberation to this wide shot. At one point we imagined shooting at 48fps, with the 52 actors moving very quickly, while the fairies moved at normal speed. We were concerned that 52 actors "acting fast" would look odd. Each suggestion put forward become more and more expensive. The option to digitally insert eight ethereal fairies and "fix it in post" was on everyone's lips. But by sticking with the problem, we eventually arrived at an acceptable, effective and inexpensive solution: teeter-totters.

The actresses hired were dancers. Putting four planks under their table, with a common fulcrum point, the actresses used their toes to delicately push themselves up and down, thus giving the illusion that they were hovering in their places rather than sitting. This solution meant we could film at 24fps.

Balancing the screenplay with the budget is a director's challenge. When the budget is fixed, the only element a director can manipulate is the script. Listen carefully to your material. It may dictate solutions for shots that cost little but enhance the story more.

Short Cuts

Responsible for the schedule, directors learn short cuts to keep the company moving at an efficient pace. Two valuable techniques are the employment of a second unit and swing crews. Both can be expensive, but the time they save translates into a savings of money so the company comes out ahead. Both part of a "B" team, they help the "A" team move faster.

The B team is the second unit, composed of cinematographer/operator, first assistant camera, clapper/loader driver and a second assistant director. During principal photography, a second unit might be assigned to shoot second camera in an action sequence, or to get shots that do not require principal actors. These shots may have been assigned to a second unit on the original schedule. They may be slop shots left over from a shoot the A team couldn't finish. These types of shots would include pick-ups, inserts, drive-bys, establishing exterior shots, etc.

Should the A team miss an insert, the second unit can put it on their "to do" list. As a small team, the second unit can move quickly, collecting shots that keep the film on schedule. Second unit can be employed for short periods, to act as second camera and collect bits and pieces of the production schedule.

As for the swing crew, they arrive on set the night before a big interior sequence. At that time they can "rough in" the lighting instruments called for by the lighting plan. Then, when the A team arrives on set the next morning, the cinematographer and gaffer complete the lighting plan, and the company is ready for principal photography much earlier than had the A team started from scratch.

Compression

Editing on set is a way of compressing a scene. During pre-production, the director envisions how he or she will shoot the movie. During production, that plan may be altered to accommodate the chaotic milieu in which a film is created. There is never enough time. Directors return home after each shooting day hoping the material will cut together in a cohesive film. One always likes to get just a little more without violating union regulations regarding overtime and turnaround. As the goal of the director is to make the best film possible, it may become necessary on occasion to go over schedule and incur the cost of turnaround penalties. It's often a trade-off. Going over a half a day to finish a scene properly may require cutting out a half-day slated to shoot another scene. As long as the director does not compromise the integrity of the screenplay, judicious cuts can be made to make the day. If made skillfully, they will not be noticed in the finished product. Sometimes the scene becomes better for the cuts.

Editing

Each moment of a film is manufactured by the production company under the leadership of a director and then shaped by the editor who uses the raw material he has been given. Film is visual storytelling, so ideally, a film should be able to be viewed without sound and have the meaning still come through. However, sound, which includes dialogue, sound effects and music, is inextricably tied to the movie experience.

An editor begins with either an assembly or rough cut. An assembly is the stringing together of all the master shots. A rough cut is the approximate editing of all the scenes and then splicing them together into a whole. In both the assembly and the rough cut, the story as a film begins to unfold. It should be noted that very few people in the world know how to watch a rough cut. Almost every director feels depressed upon screening the film for the first time.

First cuts are a bitch for a director, because it's been so many months and you put your trust in your editor and you're going to see your film assembled for the first time. You look at it and go, This is terrible. I hate it.

— Richard Donner

Walter Mirsch, in his book on editing titled *In the Blink of an Eye*, insists that continuity of action, clean matches and rhythm take a backseat to the overarching principle that the editor, like the screenwriter, actor, composer, and director, must do everything to follow the emotional arc of the story. This is important even if it means sacrificing a clean cut for a highly charged, less clean one. He calls it being "true to the emotion of the moment."

A wonderful exercise that demonstrates the power of editing is in one of Pudovkin's books on the art of montage (editing) in which he describes an experiment by his teacher, Kuleshov. You see a close up of the Russian actor Ivan Mosjoukine. This is immediately followed by a shot of a dead baby. Back to Mosjoukine again, and you read compassion on his face. Then you take away the dead baby and you show a plate of soup, and now when you go back to Mosjoukine, he looks hungry. Yet, in both cases, they used the same shot of the actor; his face was exactly the same.

Or, in the words of Hitchcock, "It [*Rear Window*] was a possibility of doing a purely cinematic film. You have an immobilized man looking out. That's one part of the film. The second part shows what he sees and the third part shows how he reacts. This is actually the purest expression of the cinematic idea." Hitchcock elaborates in an example from his film *Sabotage*: "I'm quite satisfied to let the pieces of film create the motion. For instance, in *Sabotage*, when the little boy is on the bus and he's got the bomb at his side, I cut to that bomb from a different angle every time I showed it. I did that to give the bomb a vitality of its own, to animate it. If I'd shown it constantly from the same angle, the public would have become used to the package: 'Oh well, it's only a package after all.' But what I was saying was, be careful! Watch out!"

Eventually the cut is done to the director's satisfaction. This is referred to as a director's cut. The cut should always be screened with a temporary soundtrack. The score will not have been written at this point, but the editor and/or the composer can transfer music that fits the mood of each sequence so the audience will respond as if they are watching a movie. To watch a cut without music is difficult; music makes the film come alive. After seeing it, the producers or production company may approve the cut and move on to sound design, or they might insist on further editorial changes.

Once the picture is locked, the editor and the sound designers spend weeks preparing the sound tracks for the mix. If the dialogue needs to be replaced, the actors are taken to special ADR rooms, also known as looping stages. Here the actor repeats lines that, when recorded on set, were "dirty" or unusable. The other two sound tracks are music (score, songs and on-screen music such as a band or orchestra) and effects, which are everything else, such as footsteps, doorbells, clinking glass, tire squeals and crickets.

During this phase, directors should test the film. When there is enough sound designed and a temp score has been created, some colleagues can be brought in and the film screened in its entirety. The comments from the audience will of course be helpful, especially questions about the logic of the film. The director, being so close to the film, may not realize what the audience will understand. Watching the film with an audience, not matter how small, compels the director to see it thought their eyes. It will become clear, sometimes painfully so, what scenes, moments, sound effects, and music cues work and which ones do not.

The soundtracks are broken into three major components: dialogue, effects and music. The picture editor strips all the dialogue to match to picture. During the mix, or blending of these three tracks, the dialogue is paramount. The tracks are mixed together and balanced so that each line of dialogue can be heard no matter how loud the music and/or sound effects. The remaining two tracks are given to the sound effect editing team.

The sound editing team matches the effects and music to the picture and builds the appropriate tracks. Whereas there may be three or four dialogue and music tracks that ultimately get mixed down to one each, there could be dozens of effects tracks. A final mix might be the blending of hundreds of tracks. Both effects and music make a tremendous impact on film. Directors can be torn between the heightened reality suggested by sound effects and the amplified emotion suggested by music. Sometimes it is most effective to use only sound effects; at other times a full symphonic score works best. The key decision for the director is how to balance the sounds. A prominent sound effect such as a door slam should not occur during a key line of dialogue, nor should a musical swell be cued at the same time as a strong sound effect. The result will be a muddled track. Directors will ultimately blend all three sounds carefully together to create a lush soundtrack.

As storyboarding helps move the shooting along by previsualizing the film, sound design employs a technique termed "spotting." To spot a film one marks down on mixing cue sheets exactly what sounds are played at what point in the film. For example, if at 12 minutes and 25 frames to 13 minutes and 2 frames our main character has a line of dialogue in close up, the off-screen door slam called for in the script should begin at exactly 13 minutes and 3 frames. This way the door slam will occur after the line of dialogue. If the composer wants the music to swell after the door slam, the cue for the music will be approximately 13 minutes and 5 frames. This system of spotting a film ensures that the mixing of the tracks will go smoothly.

The composer is often the last major creative collaborator to come on to the production. It is ideal to have a composer involved as early as possible so he or she can be developing themes and discussing the impact of music on the film with the director. The composer committed to the project can be helpful in pulling together a temporary music track, perhaps even using the composer's previous work. Doodling with themes for the main characters, tinkering with the relationship of different instruments to the images and exploring any source music available are all part of the composer's research process. Carol Reed discovered musician Anton Karas while location scouting Vienna bars and nightclubs during the film of *The Third Man*.

A composer, more often than not, is brought in late; often the director and editor prepare the temporary music tracks. These tracks are used to discover what style of music best supports the film. Some composers prefer to see the film for the first time without a temporary score so as not to be influenced by another musician. It takes a certain amount of time to create a score. Most films have an average of 30 to 50 minutes of score. Some films, of course, have none (Kurosawa's *High and Low*), while others take advantage of wall-to-wall music (Lucas' *Star Wars*). The more music, the longer it takes to write the score, orchestrate, transcribe the music sheets, record the music with an orchestra and then deliver to the sound editor to cut into the film.

What Does Music Do?

- It binds a picture together, particularly cuts and sequences.
- It connects shots that might not have apparent connections.
- It triggers an audience's emotional response.
- It can drive a sequence, instilling it with energy and purpose.
- It complements the drama on the screen, either by enhancement or counterpoint.
- It strengthens a character's presence through theme. If viewers can identify a character's theme, music can place the character in a scene without his presence.
- It has the ability to transport the audience to another time and place. A single instrument can be associated with a culture. When we hear bagpipes, we think of Scotland. The music of any time period has the power to carry us there immediately.
- It creates an expectation about the story. Wistful music denotes a sad or melancholy piece. A light, bubbly melody over the same footage sets the audience up for an entirely different story.

Often a director hears the score for the first time just prior to or even during the mix. It had better be top-notch, for what you hear is what you get. To ensure there is some wiggle room to shape the score, ask that the composer write more music than needed. You can delete music during the mix, but you cannot add.

The mix is the final major step in the filmmaking process. Taking around three weeks, it requires booking the mix facility long in advance, and it is expensive. As in shooting, preparation is everything. Much of the time is spent laying down the tracks, establishing a sound level and balancing the tracks. It can be an exciting, yet sometimes tedious, process. There is room for creative decisions, such as adding or dropping a music cue, finessing a dissolve from one sound to another, panning the effects behind or to the side of the auditorium, or delaying sounds by a frame or two in order to create echo or reverberation. There is no time for recutting picture.

Once the mix is complete, the timed film negative is printed and married to the track at the laboratory. Finally, a first print is made.

21 Key Issues for Editing
by Camilla Toniolo*

1. Read the script a few times, trying to understand the tone of the film. Scripts are very dry, and that's why they need a few passes. Since lots of things go wrong between the written page and what is finally committed to film, reading the script thoroughly will give you a sense of the director's vision. Although editing is mostly an intuitive craft and a lot of problem solving, it does not mean that you can be ignorant of the intentions and the hopes of the filmmaker.

2. If you can, participate to the life of the set at least one day or even a few hours. Observe the director at work and the actors as well. Mostly, editors stay away from the set to preserve their objectivity, but to be aware of the geography of a scene and the mood on the set can be helpful.

   Either way, when you are ready to start editing:

3. Screen your footage in a calm, quiet environment, with no interruptions. Take it all in and make mental notes of what you like; do not stop and start, just screen. You should do this on a scene-by-scene basis. The second time you screen a scene's footage, take notes (written or on the computer) of the following: the takes you like the most, basing your comments on performance for now, and it could be the first part of take three and the second of take one and so on; the shot you are planning to use to open the scene, to close it; and any other note you can think of. Remember that editing is very intuitive, for the first time only happens once, and those first gut reactions to how you want to put it together are precious.

4. Start putting your scene together, following a plan based on your notes. Unless you designed shots specifically for an opening, start with your master and stay on it until you can't stand it anymore. When it peaks, cut.

5. Cut into the coverage; approach the film from a slightly con-

*Used by permission.

ventional point of view. This will allow you to have a strong base from which you can take off on less conventional tangents if you want. Use the shots that you have tagged; don't delete any lines; don't overanalyze or get stuck at this precious stage of near objectivity of the material. Keep to the script and don't worry about mismatches for now.

Try to keep in mind the following:

6. Always cut for a reason, not to show you can do it. The cut has to serve the story, and the best cuts are the ones that happen when the audience wants them to happen, therefore appearing seamless.

7. Avoid confusion and avoid giving the audience a "claustrophobic" feeling. Establish your geography well with your masters and fall back onto them anytime you don't have to give a character an emotional punch by using a close-up or when someone is entering or leaving a scene.

8. Avoid boring the audience by keeping to a minimum entrances and exits. Do set up the geography of a place, but don't waste too much time doing it or you'll lose your audience.

9. Try not to show an actor waiting to act, waiting to turn or enter. Cut in motion whenever possible, as the film seems less staged that way.

10. Cut longer rather than shorter for the first time around. It's much easier to trim than to add.

11. If you get stuck on a scene and nothing that you try to do helps, on the contrary, you fall deeper and deeper into despair. Stop. Put it away. Come back the next day, screen your dailies for that scene again and give it another try. Most of the insurmountable issues you were facing will be easier to solve with some objectivity.

12. Be open to trying everything. Never apply too much rational thinking to a cut, as there are so many happy accidents. The famous saying "the only rule is that there are no rules" really applies to film editing. I am not advocating total anarchy, but you should be open and remember that everything is undoable. Having said this, here's a couple of rules:

13. Don't cut from a moving shot to a still one, and vice versa.

14. Don't cut between a shot of a certain size, say a medium, and another shot of the same character where the angle has changed

very little, say 20 degrees. This will be confusing, as the backgrounds will change, but not quite enough giving the impression of a jump.

15. When you are done assembling your scene or sequence, screen it without stopping and be aware of the impact it has on you. Jot a few notes down if it helps you, and start working at your changes right away. Different editors' styles differ on this point, but I like to work on a scene until I am completely happy with it; otherwise if I "put it on the shelf" without liking it, when I assemble all the scenes together to watch them continuously I will have too many things I am unhappy about, and it will be distracting. I still adhere to the script and use every line, but in general I am happy with all the individual cuts and the energy of the scene.

16. Once all your sequences are edited and strung together, screen the completed film.

17. At this point your notes and changes should be based on the rule: Movie first, scene second, moment third. You have to preserve what serves the entire story and its characters, and forget about those gems that may be working wonderfully in a vacuum, but bog the movie down or even hurt it.

18. At this stage you should get your dialogue track in pretty good shape, replacing off-camera lines with audible ones, cutting in easy to find sound effects such as bells, doors, traffic, etc. and adding some music, which, even if temporary, will help you and anyone else you might "screen" for look at your work without being distracted or confused.

19. Work at finessing your cut until you are happy with it, dedicating time to the parts that are troubling you. This is a very delicate process, because the balance of the story can be tipped one way or the other, and a change or deletion made in the first five minutes will affect the entire film, so you will have to review it very carefully each time. Same with the middle or last five minutes. The most important thing to remember is that, the way in which editing uses trickery and slight of hand to make the story work, to create a world, to give rhythm and a heartbeat to a flat screen is what engages an audience visually and emotionally, and not a series of perfect cuts.

20. The next is a very critical step of the editing process, because you are ready to commit to the final version of your picture cutting and to get other people involved in the completion of your film. They are unaware of what it took you to get to this version, that scene 83 may be in place of scene 1 and scene 1 is in the end crawl, so you had better seek their involvement when you are finished and happy about your cut, as it is expensive and very time consuming to undo the version that your dialogue, music and effects editors are working on.

21. So, when you are ready, sit down with your collaborators and screen the film for them, with the objective to add more layers and make your story that much more powerful.

◄◄ **7** ►►I

Command

I set a course and I steer it.
— Terry Gilliam

Filmmaking requires a siege mentality. Use authority judiciously. In pre-production, post-production and distribution, many decisions are made by committee. The director often has the final word, but there is ample time for discussion of script development, editorial choices and images for the one sheet. During production there is only one voice, that of the director.

When one imagines a general leading a charge into battle, or a sea captain fighting a gale, one can see that the person in charge is under constant pressure to make split-second decisions. Their unquestioned authority is what allows leaders to lead. Directors are given this authority; still, it's one thing to have the authority to lead, another to have the capacity and ability to do so.

A ship is a universe unto itself, like that of a motion picture production company. Overly timid people rarely make good directors. The director steers the production, like a sea captain who is given an assignment, to go from point A to point B. The ship's owner (read producer) has the financial responsibility for the journey. But the voyage itself is entrusted to the captain. The ship's owner can fire the captain, just as a producer can fire the director, but once on the high seas, the captain's word is law. During the voyage, there are good times and bad times. There is singing, there is quarreling, acts of heroism, acts of courage, smooth sailing, rough seas. A sea voyage has it all.

One does not step off a boat in mid-ocean. From stem to stern it is a single unit bobbing up and down on the ocean's tides, currents and swells. So, too, a movie set is a closed environment comprised of three concentric rings. The innermost ring is the set itself, where the camera captures the magic of performance. Just beyond is the second ring, where grips and electricians wait to adjust the camera and lights. Prop men, set dressers, make-up, hair and wardrobe assistants stand at the ready to make changes and/or repairs. Producers hover around the video tap or make hushed cell phone calls, perhaps setting up their next picture. The third concentric ring, a much larger area, consists of the grip and electric trucks, props and wardrobe vehicles, honey wagons and craft services, all of which support the two inner rings.

The set, too, is a universe unto itself. Here PAs fall in love with script supervisors, teamsters trade stock tips with grips, and prop men share stories about ideal fishing holes with studio executives. And watching over it all is the director, the ringmaster. When he or she cracks the whip, the company moves. Outside the three rings lies the public, and the vast unknown, which have no bearing on the world inside the circles.

Authority implies a chain of command. The general has his lieutenants, the captain a first mate. There are several immediate subordinates to a director, primarily the director of photography, the assistant director and the script supervisor. These three crew members are the director's chief advisors during principle photography. It is the director of photography who influences the effectiveness of the director the most. The director has direct authority over the cinematographer, who in turn has control over the grip and electric crew, representing the backbone, muscle and grease of the production. A director and cinematographer at odds would force the crew to side with the director of photography.

Time is money. If the crew moves slowly, production slows down. If the director of photography takes too much time, the director cannot make the pages that are that day's goal. Therefore, the relationship between the director and the director of photography is symbiotic. In an ideal situation, the relationship between the director and director of photography is solid and smooth, which in turn reflects on the easy relationship between the director of photography and the grip and electric crew. Being ultimately responsible for achieving each day's goal of X number of pages, if there is breakdown in this chain of command, the director may get the axe. All too often, before the director's head is placed on the chopping block, that of the cinematographer is lopped off. The speed at which the company can work is directly related to the speed at which the cinematographer is able to light the set and set the camera. He or she is usually the first to fall, even if the actual fault lies in another department, including directing.

Although the captain is the sole authority on the ship, he or she does not own the vessel. The ship's owner has the right to replace the captain in extreme circumstances. So too can a producer replace a director. It is not common, but it does occur. Try to avoid the catastrophe of being released from a film during principle photography. It is difficult to be fired from a film during production. Perhaps in pre-production a director encounters "artistic differences" with a collaborator that result in a quick exit. Principle photography is a period in which a company should not have to deal with any crisis that could have been addressed in pre-production. The firing of any principals during a shoot, including the director, cinematographer and lead actor, can only result in costly delays.

No one should be harmed in any way in the making of a motion picture. A death on set is a terrible tragedy. If the death occurs during the filming of a sequence in which all safety issues have been addressed, one is aware that accidents do happen. But if any negligence has been shown, the director must take full responsibility. Pushing the crew into long hours, shooting under less than ideal circumstances, failing to check firearms, have resulted in totally unnecessary injuries and loss of life. Making movies relies on creating illusions. There is no reason to put any actor or crew member in a life-threatening situation.

Safety and Security
- How will you load equipment into the building? If shooting in an apartment building, check if there is a freight elevator. If not, ask whether the building superintendent will allow heavy equipment in the passenger elevator.
- Does the location require any security?
- Have you made arrangements to lock up any valuables?
- If the equipment is stored in a van and parked in a lot, is the lot bonded (insured)?
- Can the equipment be left in the location overnight?
- Do you need police from the city for traffic control?
- Are you performing any stunts or tricks that would require additional safety precautions?

- Do you have additional personnel to direct traffic or hold parking spaces?
- Do you have a fire sequence that requires a standby water truck?
- Are there stunts that require a standby nurse or ambulance?

The most common grounds for asking a director to leave a production are schedule over-runs. Lets look at the numbers. If a production has a budget of $5,000,000, with one million allocated for above-the-line, and another million for post-production, production should cost three million. If the schedule is determined to be 10 five-day weeks, the company is allotted 50 days in which to shoot the movie. To spend $3,000,000 in 50 days is a daunting task, especially considering all the variables. At $60,000 a day ($6,000 an hour, $100 a minute, $1.66 a second), going over schedule has a tremendous impact on the budget. If the grand ballroom scene is scheduled to take three days, but (because of complications and delays) stretches to five days, the director is $120,000 over budget or two days behind schedule. A director who continues to go over schedule, without a viable alternative plan, runs the risk of being removed, especially if these delays occur near the start of production. If a director goes over schedule by one day after three days of principle photography, an accountant works out that the director will be over schedule 14 days on the 50th day of production. Two weeks over schedule translates to $840,000 over, almost 28 percent of the total production budget. Not good.

Alternative plans include eliminating and/or reducing scenes yet to be shot, condensing coverage of elaborate scenes, rewriting, and stealing from the post-production budget. One could damn the torpedoes and drive full speed ahead, hoping to get the footage necessary to make a winning picture before the accountants can shut you down. This method was employed in Fritz Lang's *Metropolis*, Francis Ford Coppola's *Apocalypse Now*, all Akira Kurosawa's *Seven Samurai*, all of which went way over schedule and over budget and managed to produce superior films. In each of these cases the directors remained at the helm of the project until it was completed. Other films had different outcomes for the director, hence the credit Alan Smithee.*

Each movie set carries with it the seeds of the Stockholm syndrome,

---

*Alan Smithee is the credit awarded a director who has his or her name removed from the film.

in which the captives (crew) identify with their captor (director). During shooting, the director seduces the crew into friendship. Once the shoot is over, the ransom paid, they feel that they are forgotten. As a result, many crew members and actors become depressed after a show is over and rally only when they are once again kidnapped by the movies.

No one person makes a film. Teamwork is the bedrock of production, and that is why a director's skills as a collaborator are tested. One must not overlook the contribution of other artists integral to the process. Director Sidney Lumet states that in production he is "in charge of a community that you need desperately and that needs you just as badly. That's where the joy lies, in the shared experience."

Money and fame are two major benefits that directors and stars can receive when making a picture. The remaining cast and crew make a comfortable salary and then move on to the next show. What's to motivate them beyond their paycheck? The wise director knows that involving the entire team is an intangible but genuine compensation for their long hours and hard work. Encouraging collaboration increases productivity. People appreciate it when someone pays attention to their ideas; when directors listen, it makes them feel involved and acknowledges their contribution. What better method to keep one's crew motivated than to include rather than to dominate them?

A viable idea can come from any quarter, so directors are encouraged to create an environment in which cast and crew feel their ideas are welcome and encouraged. The director wants to make the best film possible, so he or she should not feel challenged if collaborators contribute good ideas. A director who insists that his or her ideas be employed neglects an entire area of thought about the picture. "That's what intrigues me about making films," says Terry Gilliam. "You've got to listen to the people who are there. You're getting all this information. You're getting clues to the puzzle. And even though everything's scripted there's a puzzle beyond the script and that's the film itself."

At the same time one should be wary of trying to please others at the expense of the project.

There is no formula for success. But there is a formula for failure and that is to try to please everybody.
— Nicholas Ray

Chemistry as a buzz-word is bandied about often in the entertainment biz, and for good reason. It describes why people are attracted to each other. When people "click," it is said they have good chemistry. This is often a factor in the success of a picture. It may be based on personality, persona, ideology, temperament, or looks.

"Artistic differences" is an often-used legal explanation for why a contract is broken. Lawyers cannot use the phrase "bad chemistry," but, in fact, as people come together to collaborate on a project, disagreements may come to the fore. At these moments the collaborators may accept the fact that they are not compatible and bail from the project.

When casting a picture, once one of the leads has been selected, a director will often ask the actor to audition with his or her co-star. In this way the director can cast someone to play opposite the actor, who beyond their talent, "clicks" with their partner. This chemistry can be exploited in the making of the film. Many leading men and woman form a deep friendship for one another both on and off the set. Humphrey Bogart and Lauren Bacall didn't have to "act" their affection for another, nor did Ginger Rogers and Fred Astaire, John Wayne and Maureen O'Sullivan, or Myrna Loy and William Powell.

Good chemistry is golden. It is not a line item on a budget, but it can be seen on the screen. One hopes to "get the budget up on the screen" when making a picture. When Mel Brooks makes a film, the atmosphere he creates is great fun and full of collaboration, and the comic touches that we see in the theater are a direct result of chemistry. Yet there is no budget figure for fun.

Many directors throughout history have surrounded themselves with a company or stable of actors and crew members with whom they like to work. The director takes this ensemble of collaborators from picture to picture. A cast and crew, working on picture after picture, develops shorthand for communication, which speeds up the work. Also, these collaborations often turn up a unique artistic melding of an actor and director. This has been the case with the collaboration of Akira Kurosawa and Toshiro Mifune, John Ford and John Wayne, Tod Browning and Lon Chaney, Martin Scorsese and Robert De Niro, to name a few.

Collaboration begins with the formation of the team. Casting and crewing correctly will contribute greatly to the success of the endeavor. A director who possesses a good script and gathers a solid cast and crew is in an ideal position to make a successful film. This is why directors gravitate to known quantities: experienced writers, well-known actors and familiar crews. Making a film is such an incredible gamble that you need any advantage you can get.

There are certain prerequisites a director needs to command a cast, one of which is to know the script inside and out. Sidney Lumet says it best, "It is important as a director I understand each and every line." Actors will push themselves if they feel the director is integral to the process. But directors are human and prone to mistakes. Feel free to admit error. Since the director spends all day making decisions, some will need adjusting. Accept the fact, make the adjustment, and move on.

The shooting plan includes a production schedule. This schedule balances the budget, the contract dates for cast, and location availability. Each department head, including the director, has a say on what goes into the schedule. Although the production manager and the first assistant director manage the schedule, the director has the final word. The completed schedule indicates how many pages and what scenes are to be filmed on any given day. The director is responsible for making all the pages scheduled for each day. It is not, however, a perfect system. Hollywood has been referred to as a dream factory, but dreams have little truck with logic. A director is shooting a script, not a schedule. So the question becomes how to improvise, juggle and manipulate the schedule without projecting an overrun to the producers.

When bees find a field, they do not keep the information to themselves. Instinctively, they rush back to the colony to perform a dance announcing the discovery. So, too, must a director communicate with the hive. For example, if a director gives up on using a dolly and wants a crane on the set instead, he or she must go back to the hive and do the crane dance. But if the director fails to do the crane dance, the crew will have a dolly waiting instead. And if the director throws a tantrum, he or she will be stung, if not by the crew, then surely by the time and money wasted because of a communication breakdown.

Kurosawa was a great one for promoting verbal communication. He stated that a director talks through the screenplay, barks orders and discusses options during production, argues with the editor over each edit, and offers words of wisdom and support as the film is nursed out onto the marketplace. Kurosawa would have loved directing a silent film, as he could have shouted out directions while cameras were churning away. Some directors employed a live orchestra when making a silent film, to play just off set during the filming to create a mood for the actors. A director has other means of communicating besides speech. There is drawing, writing, sign language, grunting, even nudging, if need be. They can occur through production meetings, storyboards, photographs and call sheets, to name a few.

If you want results, communication should be precise. It's not "place the camera over there"; it's "Place the camera where a 50 mm lens will hold a close up on one character and the character at the door will be slightly out of focus." It is frustrating, having to adjust during production as a result of poor communication.

Peter de Vries said, "I love being a writer. What I can't stand is the paperwork." Well, he would have hated being a director because moviemaking requires a tremendous amount of paperwork, much of which is duplicated and distributed to multiple parties. There is the screenplay, revisions, rewrites, budget, contracts, production breakdowns, production reports, camera reports, lab reports, call sheets, production schedules, day out of days, storyboards, the lined script and memos. Lots of memos. Read *Memo from David O. Selznick* to know how pervasive the memo is.

In all written communication, bad spelling or punctuation and incorrect grammar will gain you little respect. It may even keep you from striking a deal if backers think you are uneducated. Reading Strunk and White's *Elements of Style* will guarantee an improvement in one's writing. A carefully worded memo, script notes, a letter to a vendor to consider product placement will get better results with proper English.

The production meeting is the proper venue to disseminate information. It is recommended a full production meeting with department heads be convened every Monday morning and Friday evening during each week of pre-production. If necessary, continue this practice during principle photography. The Monday meeting establishes goals for the coming week, while the Friday meeting is a wrap-up of the week's activities. During this meeting the key challenges facing the production are discussed in detail to keep each department up to speed. Nobody wants any surprises when making a film.

One can only imagine the response at the production meeting for Hitchcock's film *The Birds* when the crew read in the script, "A flock of birds chases and attacks a group of school children." This is not a case of calling in the local bird wrangler, giving him the date of the shoot and to telling him to show up with a bunch of birds. The birds in *The Birds* needed to be trained months prior to shooting (for which, presumably, Hitchcock wrote a detailed, well-composed memo to set up).

In a production meeting, the script is examined line-by-line, scene-by-scene, with each department sharing insights and information about how to best affect the director's vision. Ideas are discussed, recorded and either embraced or discarded. Directors may not participate in some of the more technical details, but they have the final word on each important decision. Every solution has an impact on the budget, schedule and of course the quality of the final product. What is noteworthy in this triangle of interconnectedness is the delicate ripple effect of each choice. An insight may solve a particular problem that the director encounters in the script, but it may be expensive and/or take additional time to shoot (see Chapter 9: Luck).

Even though directors surround themselves with the best production crews available for the budget, they should also know a great deal about the function and resources of each department. Alfred Hitchcock was famous for his knowledge of the craft and was constantly pushing the envelope to blend ideas with innovative cinematic techniques. Shooting a film in one continuous take (*Rope*) or on a small boat (*Lifeboat*) are two of his many experiments. Hitchcock's films are peppered with engaging cinematic techniques that he and his crew invented to propel the story. The glass of milk lit from inside the glass in *Suspicion* or the oversized revolver in *Spellbound* are two examples.

Let's take the scene in Alfred Hitchcock's film *Suspicion* in which Cary Grant carries a glass of milk up the stairs to his wife. If, in an early production meeting, Hitchcock said to his crew that for dramatic purposes he would like the milk to have a luminous effect, their collective minds would begin whirring. Although a challenge directed primarily at the electric department, the directive could be solved by any member of the team, including the director. How about a bright follow pin-spot? This solution would require elaborate lighting and split-second timing on the part of the follow spot technician and the actor.

During the production meeting, the production manager and assistant director begin to calculate the time and money necessary to light the milk. Perhaps Hitchcock is asked to reconsider; after all, the audience will surely understand that the character is carrying milk to his wife, possibly laced with poison. The director says no; this is an important detail that requires an effective touch. More possible solutions are kicked around. Finally an ingenious solution (for its time) is presented. A small light bulb will be placed inside the glass, giving the milk an extra kick of brightness on the film. To avoid trailing an extension cord up the stairs behind the actor, the lamp was powered by a battery pack strapped to Cary Grant's back. Creative solutions like this are found because many people collaborated in the discussions and the final decision.

The director consults with the assistant director at lunch to review the plan for the following day. This plan is sent to the production office coordinator, who types up the call sheets and makes copies for the entire cast and crew. Each shooting day is neatly condensed into a call sheet, handed out at wrap, which indicates everything required for the next day's shooting. Information distilled onto this one piece of paper includes: the call times for actors and crew, what scenes are to be shot and in what order, special equipment requests, a map and directions to the location. At the end of each day, if you have communicated clearly and often, and left no one out of the loop, you will have a tightly organized and very productive crew on the morrow.

There are several forms of communication. Storyboards, for instance, are invaluable for keeping everyone on the same page, or frame, to be duplicated by the camera. Directors vary in the number of storyboards they require for a picture. Some directors want every frame previsualized in a storyboard, while others may not employ them at all. Most directors fall somewhere in between. A director will certainly have a stunt or special effect sequence boarded. To guarantee safety and to use time efficiently, stunts cannot be improvised; each angle, the estimated length of the shot, and the various camera positions are detailed in the storyboards. The assistant director, stunt coordinator, stunt person and director of photography can scrutinize the boards and compare notes until the shot is ready to be photographed. Storyboards eliminate guesswork and keep production rolling.

The precision with which directors must marry live action with post-production visual effects demands they storyboard all special effect shots and sequences. In this way the set and the post-production house have fluid communication through the storyboards. Notations accompany the storyboards back and forth between the special effects house, the set and the laboratory to ensure a perfect frame.

Photos taken by the script supervisor are used to maintain picture continuity. After each sequence, the script supervisor takes a snap of the set. This allows for duplication of the location should the company return. Photos of the actors are also shot, sometimes by the script supervisor as well as the costumer. These pictures are kept on a set to keep track of what the actor is wearing in each scene. All these images become one of the many forms of communication on set.

To be in the middle of the intense moment of shooting a scene while at the same time feeling one's body floating above the chaos, objectively analyzing the progress of the picture, illustrates the schizophrenic nature of directing. It's as if a director has two heads, one to design the moment, another to design the whole. As Alfred Hitchcock said, "Many directors are conscious of the over-all atmosphere on the set, whereas they should be concerned with what's going to come up on the screen."

Richard Attenborough thinks objectivity is a crucial quality in directing: "Obviously the most important talent, it seems to me if one uses that word, that a director acquires is his ability, during the shooting of the picture, to be able to maintain and contain in his mind, in his eye, the entity, the whole, the shape, the tempo, the graph, the thrust forward, etc. This applies to tempo; this applies to emotion; this applies to character development and everything else."

In the novel *1984* George Orwell invents the concept of *doublethink*. *Doublethink* means to hold two contradictory beliefs in one's mind simultaneously, and accept both of them. The notion of doublethink and duality is applicable to film directing. The director stands near the camera, calls "Action!" and while the drama unfolds, thinks both these thoughts simultaneously: Is this the right piece of the puzzle? and Will it play in Peoria?

Disassociating oneself from the heat of the moment requires emotional willpower. To step back affords the director an opportunity to set the stage clearly, in order to shape the sequence. Ask the script supervisor prior to each shot, "What does this shot cut from, and what will it cut to?"

A director often gives 110 percent to the show, which is why switching gears is emotionally demanding. Besides all the creative decisions that bear on the outcome of the picture, the director also acts as arbitrator in cases requiring impartiality. Evenhandedness means seeing both sides in an argument yet handing down a decision that will keep the company moving forward. Should the company run to a cover set? Should the walls be painted green? Should the car be moving or standing still? The final decisions always rest with the director. It's one of the few jobs in life where you have all the power and all the responsibility. But you must try to remain objective at every turn in the process.

To be in the moment and observe the moment detachedly is much like patting your head and rubbing your tummy at the same time. Jean Cocteau, ever humble, once said, "I am not a real director and probably never shall be. I get too interested in what is happening. I begin to watch the action as though it were a play. I become a part of the audience and then I forget all about the continuity." Being present during the production period is akin to visiting a magic kingdom. And in his diary on the making of *Beauty and the Beast* he noted, "I ask myself whether or not these exhausting days may not be the sweetest of my life. For they are filled with friendship, harmless quarrels, laughter and contain moments when we seem to hold fleeting time in our hands."

Being human, even Jean Cocteau was often plagued with self-doubt. The pressure to produce excellent work in the brief period of production easily erodes confidence. "There are times when I am ashamed of imposing discipline on them (the cast and crew) which they accept only out of confidence in me. Such confidence destroys my own makes me fear I am not worthy of theirs." Directors with strong and confident demeanors rarely need to exert their authority. Despite many raging egos trampling over the set, a calm director who knows he or she is in control can be very effective.

Pre-production addresses and answers the questions that are asked before commencing principle photography. In the same way a director's contract contains everything to enable him or her to function easily. Wrestling with the production office for "perks" that could have been negotiated before principle photography is time consuming and aggravating. Laundry, car service, per diem and special meals are easily negotiated as part of a contract.

Directors should embrace the principle of anticipating problems and solving them before they become predicaments. While no one has a crystal ball to see into the future, past experience opens our eyes to what might lie ahead.

Let's take the example of a director who does not want the actors to attend dailies. If an actor is barred from the screening room it may cause ill will, or even an argument. The actor may win the argument, watch the dailies and voice objections about the lighting or the coverage (which is why a director might consider this ban). If, however, the director's contract has a clause or rider put into it, stating no actor is allowed to dailies, this information will be known by all parties long before cameras roll.

It's terrific when a producer and director work like a well-oiled machine. There are some noted collaborations between directors and cinematographers, or directors and actors. But the relationship on set between producer and director can sometimes become strained. The producer has accomplished a great deal by bringing the project to fruition. Then the reigns are handed over to the director to make the film. If all goes well, the producer can settle into the role of problem solver. The fewer the problems, the less the producer has to do. But people in the film business, especially entrepreneurial types, enjoy being actively involved. And since they have the authority to fire the director, a producer might abuse his or her position, thus causing unwarranted delays.

Most productions have multiple producers. If several producers are on set during a difficult sequence and start to hound the director, the director is compelled to stop everything to address the concerns of the producers. This is an awkward situation in which the cast and crew stop working. They might begin to question the director's ultimate authority. Even worse, time is ticking away while the director negotiates in heated and unnecessary conversation. This is called "double teaming" the director. How to avoid it? Put it in your contract. No more than one producer on set at a time. If two producers come on set and harangue you, simply remind them they are in violation of their contract. It is easy to be without ego if one creates a harassment-free environment.

Terry Gilliam gets high praise from Brad Pitt, who appreciates his leadership: "When I think about Terry [Gilliam], besides being a genius and the visual artist he is, is that the man has no ego. He really doesn't, and he's so aware of what he knows and he's so aware of what he doesn't know." Remember, he who has learned to obey will know how to command.

Guidelines to Help a New Director through a First Project
Make It Clear Who Is In Charge. There must be a leader and a decision maker on the set. The director should know what he or

she wants and be able to communicate his or her desires to others. The best way to insure this is to be prepared. *Do your homework* before you walk on the set.

Treat All Crew Members With Respect. In most cases, the crew (and cast) is working for little or no pay. Remember that they are all part of a team and that everyone on the team is important.

Know What Everyone Does. If you understand the value of every position, you can evaluate what you really need for a particular production. Know also what every piece of equipment does.

Clarify Job Requirements. If crew members hold more than one position apiece, be sure that job requirements don't conflict, and clearly establish who will do what. There shouldn't be any assumptions on the set; you don't want to hear, "I thought *he* was taking care of that." An effective crew should be able to accommodate any demands asked of it.

⏮ **8** ⏭

Pace

Everything comes to him who hustles while he waits.
— Thomas A. Edison

Pace is an important property particular to the performing arts. In this chapter pace has two meanings: the rhythms of the film as dictated by the screenplay, and the tempo of a day's work as set by the director. Often these two are in sync and play off one another; at other times they are at odds. What's important is that directors recognize and respond to them accordingly.

Pace in a film is important because the success or failure of a project in many ways is dependent on it. When the credits roll or the lights come up in a theater, you, as an audience member experiencing a well-paced film, can't believe it's over. You are satisfied. You are thrilled. You want more. You got your money's worth.

Going to the water fountain during a film, refilling your popcorn, looking at your watch, glancing around to see who is in the theater, checking out the sticky substances on the floor — all are tell-tale signs of a film's poor pace. A poorly paced film is a struggle to sit through. Even if the story is interesting, the acting engaging, the photography and the sets captivating, without proper pacing an audience may become antsy. It is this ephemeral quality of pace that hooks the audience and reels them into the final reel.

What is pace? It is rhythm, volume, negative space, speed and intensity all rolled into one. Like comedy, which illustrates the need for pace, it either works or it doesn't work. Comedy competently illustrates this point. A joke, or a funny bit of business, depends on the way it is told or performed. The precision of comedy relies on effective tempo. A joke told too slowly is boring and the listener may leap ahead and guess the punch line. A monotone is boring. If the speaker laughs all the way through the story, or tells it too fast, it is ruined. Storytelling is an art in which the manner of telling is as important as the story itself.

A conductor blends the art and craft of music into a performance. Many of the practical and psychological factors that go into a musical concert echo those in film. A conductor, like a film and television director, must know a great deal about music and each of the instruments playing notes.

A conductor does not change any of the notes in the score of the composer. The conductor interprets the notes on the page into a harmonious event, a concert. So, too, a theater director uses the text verbatim in mounting a play. A film director, however, assembles all the elements made available, with the screenplay as a blueprint, and turns them into moving pictures. The note on the score and the sound made by the musician is always the same. Each actor interprets the lines in a play in his own way, but the text itself will vary. In film, the image a director creates from the words indicated on the screenplay page takes into account myriad additional details that will affect the final image.

The conductor of an orchestra has particularly close ties to a film director in regard to pace. Terms such as *overture, rhythm, tempo, volume, modulation, pitch, rest, crescendo, decrescendo, harmony, dissonance, cacophony, stinger* and *coda* are a few examples of language employed by both a film director and a musical conductor.

An overture is a short preliminary movement in a larger work in which the major musical themes are introduced. The beginning of a film, often the title sequence, is a wonderful opportunity to introduce characters and themes. Who can forget the sense of isolation in the long aerial tracking shot that opens Kubrick's *The Shining*? Or the bandits overlooking the village in Kurosawa's *Seven Samurai* discussing when they should invade and pillage the town? Robert Altman's film *The Player* opens with a lengthy title sequence in one shot that introduces the main characters and the inciting incident, a death threat to the studio production chief.

In music, rhythm is a regular pattern formed by a series of notes of differing duration and stress. A waltz, a march, a tango or a ballad each has its own rhythm. A waltz is 3:4 time, a march 4:4, etc. These are precise rules that can be applied to film directing. To ask an actor to waltz across the room is very different from asking the actor to march across the same space. In Billy Wilder's *Some Like It Hot*, our two main characters, dressed as women to escape the Mafia, watch with wonder as Marilyn Monroe walks away from them demonstrating a gyrating rhythm in her hips that begins to give them an idea about how to act like a woman.

Tempo is the rate of speed of movement or performance. Knowing the entire screenplay so well, the director can feel if a line or an action is too fast or too slow to fit into the overall picture. Asking an actor or camera operator to change speeds guarantees a different pace will be imbedded into each beat of a scene. The variations in film speed in *The Matrix* alter the tempo often several times within a given scene. It is the stitching together in editing of all these beats that reveals the ultimate pace of the film, a treasure map known only to the director.

The director's first consideration with volume is the microphones. Microphones are placed in various parts of the set and/or on the actor (radio microphones). If actors speak too softly for the recorder to pick up, they'll have to speak louder. If the lines are to be whispered, it should be a stage whisper. Conversely, if the recorder needle is pinned in the red because an actor speaks too loud, the director asks for a softer delivery. The force with which an actor speaks carries with it delicate shades of performance. A booming voice can denote strong character, a thin voice is weak, an angry voice with volume is what a bully might use, whereas an angry character who whispers seems sinister. Consider the explosive volume of the gun shot in *Shane* and Brandon De Wilde's subsequent reaction. The director, George Stevens, Jr., wanted to make it a strong story point that guns are powerful and need to be used wisely.

In William Wyler's *The Best Years of Our Lives*, Dana Andrews' character enters an aviation graveyard toward the end of the film. The music segues from the previous scene in a major key as Dana Andrew's father reads a letter concerning the brave deeds of his son during the war. As the character enters the nose of an airplane, the music shifts from a major to a minor key, foreshadowing the purging of his ghosts. Modulation is a passing from one key or tonality to another by means of a regular melodic or chord progression. The constant variations on speed, rhythm and volume are what keep the piece interesting. It's why monotone induces sleep. Directors strive to keep their audiences awake and involved in the story. Keeping the experience "lively" means variety, in the shot selection, performance levels, and pace.

Pitch consists of seven tones in fixed relationship to a tonic, having a characteristic key signature and being; since the Renaissance, the structural foundation of the bulk of Western music has been tonality. In film, one could say the tonality is the theme of the story. Many scores attribute a theme to a specific character or mood. In *Casablanca*, when we see Humphrey Bogart's character, a few strains of *As Time Goes By* suggest nostalgia and his love for Ingrid Bergman's character. Bernard Herrmann's score in *Psycho* has the violins play at a very high pitch to match the intensity of the shocking murder in the shower scene.

Rest in music is an interval of silence. Not enough can be said of the rest or pause in performance, analogous to empty space in art. This empty, or negative, space is important to the appreciation of the whole picture. The director Peter Brook titled his groundbreaking book on directing *The Empty Space*. The dramatic pause, the space between words, the looks that occur between people, silence, all play an important role in the expression of drama. Do not underestimate its power, especially in the establishment of a rhythm in a scene. An excellent example comes from Kurosawa's masterpiece film *Ikiru*. In an early scene, just after the main character has learned that he has cancer and possibly only six months to live, the director has him walking in a busy street with construction going on in the background, but he has turned the sound completely off. By resting the soundtrack, Kurosawa allows us, the audience, to empathize with the plight of the main character.

Crescendo and decrescendo are passages played with a gradual increase or decrease in volume or intensity. The concept of the "build" is best expressed in a crescendo. Directors seek means to build to a climax. They layer beat upon beat, which become more and more intense, louder or softer, faster or slower. This brings a beat, a scene or an entire film to a logical and satisfying conclusion. To use another example from George Stevens, Jr.'s, *Shane*, the scene in which the two main characters bond over the physical removal of a stubborn stump makes for a dynamic crescendo. Editing, sound effects and music are used to build to the climax of the stump being yanked from the earth.

Harmony is a combination of sounds considered pleasing to the ear. A film director looks for moments when actors can play off one another, or the camera complements an actor by creating the visual equivalent of musical harmony. In the opening of Hitchcock's *Strangers on a Train*, the intercutting between two pairs of shoes is akin to a musical complement or harmony.

Dissonance and cacophony are harsh, disagreeable combinations of sound, the antithesis of harmony. The tension created by disagreeable sounds or visual moments cries out for relief, making the shift to harmony all the more satisfying, once again creating variety. The progression from major chords to minor chords exemplifies this tension, variety and satisfaction. The equivalent in cinematography would be a canted or dutch angle. When the camera is titled slightly, the audience has an uneasy feeling. Carol Reed used this technique to great effect in his classic film *The Third Man*.

A stinger is a sharp conclusion. Someone opens the door. Backlit, we see the prodigal son. A sharp chord on the piano is a stinger. In film it's called a button, a way to close a moment or a scene. When Rhett Butler in *Gone with the Wind* says, "Frankly; my dear, I don't give a damn," that is the button to the scene. A stinger.

A passage at the end of a movement or composition that brings it to a formal close is called a coda. It occurs in films after the climax. It is referred to in literature as the denouement. Hitchcock, in *Psycho*, chose to put in a ten-minute coda with the psychiatrist explaining why Norman Bates killed his mother and kept her body. Hitchcock felt the movie's subject was so disturbing that it would need a lengthy coda to allow the audience time to absorb the story and to "cool down." In *Casablanca* the climax of the film occurs on an airfield with spies and lovers racing for a plane. When Humphrey Bogart and Claude Rains walk out onto the tarmac after the takeoff, the coda to the movie is the line, "I think this is the beginning of a beautiful relationship."

The pace of the film is built into each beat, each scene, and only when strung together is the rhythm of the whole appreciated. Therefore, the director, as the principal audience on set, determines, shapes and approves the pace of the scenes. To accomplish this, the director must know the script intimately and be able to approximate pace prior to production. This is particularly important as most films are shot out of sequence. To shoot scene 95 on day three, and have it naturally build upon scene 94, which may be shot weeks later, means a director must orchestrate the action to fit into a grand scheme. There are far too many examples of films that begin with a knockout, fast-paced, highly charged opening, only to fall flat for the remaining 80 minutes. Watching a high-energy film that doesn't deliver is unsatisfying. Films can start slowly and then build up a head of steam. No one ever walks out on the first 20 minutes of a movie. As William Shakespeare once said, "To climb steep hills requires slow pace at first." Even a roller coaster ride begins with the clickety-clack of the cars being pulled up to the highest point of the ride before making the first of many stomach-wrenching plunges.

This is not true with television. Because directors must grab their audience before the first commercial break, the opening of a dramatic show is frequently fast paced and highly charged. The trick is knowing how to maintain that pace or to segue to calmer moments in order to build again to another dramatic climax.

Editing plays an integral role in the final pacing of the film. If an actor on stage says a funny line and the audience laughs, the actor with the next line knows to pause before continuing, so the laughter won't drown out the dialogue. On a film set, if an actor says a funny line, there is no laughter. The director senses it, counts the appropriate number of beats, and then cues the next bit of business. This is why it is imperative directors be allowed to screen their films for an audience while they are cutting: in order to recognize moments when a theater audience might have an audible reaction.

In the days of vaudeville, comedian's patter used a rhythm that built to a tag line, climax or "button." This early-20th-century performance (which made a neat transition to film in the 1930s and then disappeared from the theater) was used by Samuel Beckett in his classic play *Waiting for Godot*. The manner in which the patterns of speech are written for Estragon and Vladimir are most effective when performed in this vaudeville style. Another example of effective patter is the opening scene of Preston Sturges' film *Sullivan's Travels*. A single eight-minute take of extremely witty and rapid-fire dialogue (punctuated with pauses for dramatic effect) required high-energy blending of script, acting and camera.

Pace is inherent in the screenplay. A talented director can read a script and determine if it's a good story and if it is well paced. Many films have great beginnings, dynamic endings with in betweens that are ordinary. Only with proper pace, creating momentum toward a satisfying conclusion, can a director help a film be successful.

Following on the heels of pace is the need for patience, like the forbearance of Job. Amidst the mayhem and organized chaos, the director must be like the calm at the eye of the storm. Waiting can be frustrating or rewarding depending on how directors choose to use their time. Margaret Thatcher's way of thinking went like this, "I am extraordinarily patient, provided I get my own way in the end."

"Hurry up and wait" is a phrase common to filmmaking. It applies primarily to the time it takes to light a sequence, although it can also refer to set-up time for hair, make-up, set dressing, etc. The sun, clouds and inclement weather can delay a shoot. These are legitimate reasons to wait. Then there are the illegitimate causes. Cast or crew members arriving on set late or key pieces of equipment and props lost or left at base camp.

The virtue of patience may best be discovered on a movie set. With the amount of money spent during production, it is difficult to not to want to push forward at all cost. There is always a correct time to push. If the director insists on shooting (which is his or her right), the result may be unacceptable. Knowing just when to call for a shot is something learned through experience. One of the primary functions of the assistant director is to monitor and propel set procedure. A professional film crew knows how and when to perform their tasks. The assistant director provides the grease to ensure that progress on the set is made quickly and efficiently.

The director arrives on set and works with the actors and the director of photography to shape the day's photography. Once a shot has been designed, the director turns the set over to the first assistant director. The assistant director's job at this point is to make sure that the minute the director leaves the set until he or she returns to call the shot, the time is used efficiently. The first thing the assistant director does is ask the director of photography and the art director, "How long? How long will it take to light the set and how long will it take to dress it?" These two key department heads then estimate the time it will take to prepare the set for the sequence.

Next, the assistant director determines to whom the set belongs first. To have grips, electric, cameramen, cinematographers, set dressers, art directors and prop persons racing about all at the same time is a recipe for chaos. Based on experience and terrific people skills, the assistant director determines an order that allows specific crews on the set at certain times. For example, though the electric department is more often first on the set, should a practical lamp need to be wired, the set dresser will first provide the instrument before the electrician increases the wattage, or it might happen that set painters should have the set first to allow their paint to dry while hot lights are placed.

The director of photography tells the assistant director how long it will take for the set to be ready. If the director of photography says it will take one hour to light the set, the assistant director works toward that goal. The grip and electric department is in full swing during this prep period, rolling in cable (power), laying and leveling track, setting lenses, marking for focus, flagging flares, changing bulbs, wetting streets and flying in instruments. The assistant director will ask at 15-minute intervals if the schedule is holding, because at the end of an hour, the assistant director will want to begin photography. This is critical, because a problem for the director of photography may suddenly arise that requires time not previously calculated.

The assistant director monitors the progress of the set while coordinating the time for the return of the actors. To have the set ready with no actors present is as inefficient as having the actors ready on a set still being lit. Arranging for the harmonious marriage of actors and set in the same state of preparedness is the mark of a good assistant director.

The actors, under the watchful eyes of the second assistant director, are hustled from make-up, to hair, to wardrobe. Once they are ready, they may go to any number of quiet areas, such as a greenroom or a trailer. This quiet time is ideal for the director to engage the actor or actors in discussion about the pending scene. Some actors use these opportunities to run (memorize) lines, which can be done with the other actors, script supervisor and/or director. Time also needs to be allotted for the special effects supervisor, working with the costume dresser, to prepare the actor's wardrobe if the shot calls for any special effect, such as squibs (blood packs from gun shots).

Directors take this time to study the details of the set, review the planned photography, and even stand in for lighting. What better way to be at the eye of the storm, in the actor's spot, than to stand in for lighting. A director might retire to his or her chair just off set and study the script. This time can be spent reviewing the upcoming scene or planning for future set-ups. When the assistant director determines the time is right, he or she calls for the actors to come to the set. All is primed and ready. The assistant director then turns the reins back to the director. After a final run-through, the assistant director calls the shot and, with a little luck, magic happens.

Murphy's Law features prominently in film production (see Chapter 9: Luck). The scenario above is the ideal, and life doesn't always go so smoothly. The weather, for example, is fickle, unpredictable, and uncontrollable. Directors need a tremendous amount of patience when it comes to the weather. The following are quotes from the diary of Jean Cocteau during the making of *Beauty and the Beast:*

> Will we have sun? Will we have a camera that works? Will something else go wrong? I will try and get some sleep and wait. Wait. That's how it is with films.
>
> Tue am 7 o'clock. First thing I look at the sky. It is overcast! Now we are going to be held up for days, with the actors all ready, and able to do nothing but play cards.
>
> Patience is essential to this profession. You must wait. Always wait. Wait for the car that's coming to fetch you. Wait till the lights are fixed. Wait till the camera's ready. Wait while branches are nailed to their supports. Wait for sunlight. Wait for the scene painters. Wait. Wait till it's developed. Wait for the sound track to be married to the picture. Wait till the projection rooms is free. Wait while the projectionist changes the lamps that have just fused. Wait. Wait. Wait.

Lighting a film set is complicated. Unwanted shadows and flares are too often discovered after a final run through. If a major lighting adjustment is required, the actors are sent back to their rest areas. This is unfortunate because waiting may dispel the actor's energy or shatter concentration.

Painting with light is what a director of photography does best. But all directors should be able to assess a set for illumination. A director of photography who asks for additional time is at odds with the director's prime directive to "make the pages." If a set is lit to the director's satisfaction, he or she can, by rights, start shooting the scene. Of course an impatient director, demanding photography begin, while the actors are not quite lit, renders the dailies unusable.

The art department plays an important role in the delivery of actors to the set. The assistant director tracks the progress of each of the art departments to ensure timely delivery of the actors. These include make-up, hair, wardrobe, and stunts. Make-up is easily calculated. Men need very little time; women need more. A company that takes the time to perform make-up, hair and wardrobe tests during pre-production informs the assistant director of the approximate time required for each actor to prepare. When prosthetics are involved, from a simple scar or elongated nose, to creature masks and dangling eyeballs, timing of the make-up becomes critical.

Special prosthetic make-up necessitates an actor to be in a make-up chair for hours at a time before called to set. The first assistant director considers this fact when making the schedule. In some cases, the assistant director will insist the make-up artist, a second assistant director, a driver and the actor arrive on set hours before the crew call. The same is true for hair. Normal hair and the maintaining of continuity of hair can be planned. Once fake facial hair or wigs come into play, additional time is scheduled.

Dressing in costume can be done quickly. Special attention is given to costumes that need to be scored, distressed, prepared for squibs or perform any story point. An example of a wardrobe-related story point would be if a character playing an army lieutenant has his epaulettes ripped off by his commanding officer, or if a stout actor bends over and his pants need to split at a particular moment called for in the script. In both these examples, the costume is prepared so the epaulettes snap off easily and the pants are pre-ripped and loosely sewn back up, so the tear is noticeable.

The stunt department works hand in glove with the art department. When an actor perform his or her own stunt, the stunt department provides special preparations and precautions. These range from flame retardant (if an actor is required to work near or with fire) to a jerk harness (a character is hit by a shotgun blast). But a stunt player doubling for the actor performs most stunts. These stunt men and women must first be dressed and made-up to look as much like the character as possible. Even though the action is fast and the stunt far enough from the camera to hide the fact that it is not the actor, careful attention is given to the duplication process.

Extremely hazardous stunts, such as working with fire, entail special wardrobe, gloves, wigs and even helmets to guarantee the safety of the stunt person. This is an especially important arena in which to be patient. There have been cases when a director has called for an unrehearsed shot with stunts prematurely. Impatience has resulted in injury and even death. Since the director is the highest authority on set, injury and death are always the responsibility of the person in charge.

When shooting in a foreign country it is imperative to keep an ear tuned to the local phrase for "no problem," because it is at that precise moment the director knows he or she is in trouble. "No problem" has two definitions. One: the speaker is trying to assuage any concerns by implying the problem is easily taken care of. Two: the speaker finds your problem is not his or her problem, in other words, "not my problem." In either case, prick up your ears when these words are spoken, just to be on the safe side. Should you shoot in the Comoros, the local phrase for "no problem" is "kavatsi tabu."

The other definition of pace is that of the director's instrument, his or her body and voice as a guiding light. As the true audience of one on set, the director's inner clock is linked to that of the production and the screenplay. A tired, exhausted, lethargic director will produce tired, exhausted, and lethargic dailies. Conversely, a hyperanimated, Ritalin-prone director might produce hyperanimated, Ritalin-prone dailies.

On a 50-day shoot the director should be at the same level of energy (to guarantee a consistent result) on day 50 as he or she was on day one. As I mentioned in Chapter 5: Health, many first-time directors burn themselves out by day 10 of a difficult shoot. This results in either their being replaced, or producing less energetic and focused dailies in the latter part of the shoot.

Directors need to maintain not only their health during a shoot but their energy level as well. As the leader of the company, the director needs to inspire the cast and crew. Most of this inspiration comes from the director's energy. When it flags, so too does that of the company. Do whatever is necessary to maintain it. Take naps. Eat wisely. Avoid drugs and alcohol. Drink plenty of water. Laugh. Remember the Tortoise and the Hare: Slow and steady wins the race. Or as John Ford used to say, "Making a film is like a trip out west in the old days. The director looks forward to the journey, but after the thirst, bumpy wagons and desperadoes, you just want to get to your destination alive."

Luck

Every director will tell you that both good and bad luck play a decisive role in filmmaking. It is such an integral part in the process that directors need to know what to do with it when it hits them.

There are varying degrees of luck. Murphy's Law, obviously thought up by cynical engineers, states, "If something can go wrong, it will." But we don't often hear the optimist's version that luck can run in our favor, too. How else can we explain why, when an actor bails on the shoot, another is cast who turns out to be much better than the original? Or why certain people get into political office? Cocteau said, "I believe in luck: how else can you explain the success of those you dislike?"

There are those of course who do not believe in luck, but see the turn of any event as fate. No matter how you interpret it, the event has still turned. Was it bad luck that director Terry Gilliam had difficulty raising adequate funds to make *Monty Python and the Holy Grail*? If he had raised the money the Python Troupe originally planned, you would have seen quite a different movie. "The success of *Holy Grail*," states Gilliam, "is due to the fact we didn't have the money to make a mediocre epic. Given the time and the money we would have been mediocre. But because we didn't, we had to come up with silly ideas, which in the end, proved to be much more interesting."

Luck favors those with "a prepared mind," as Louis Pasteur once said. It happens when you least expect it. When Cocteau saw how poorly a set had been designed, he said to the art director, "I thought it was almost a godsend that the camera had broken down, for your set looked as though it had been made out of handkerchiefs and walking sticks."

It's one thing to happen upon luck, but it's quite another to head it off at the pass. This is why pre-production is so critical to the success of a production. A stitch in time in solving a problem in pre-production saves nine on set. And the time it would have taken to address that problem can be used to solve any unforeseen dilemmas.

Such as weather. Nowhere else is luck more of a factor in filmmaking than with the weather. Cocteau wondered, "It's strange that an enterprise as expensive as making films can be entirely at the mercy of the barometer." Beyond the control of any director, weather will play a role unless the film is scripted to be shot entirely interior. The sun is bright, and then it goes behind clouds. But for how long? It starts to drizzle. Will it last? For how long? What if it starts to pour? Can the scene be rewritten to be played in the rain? Can the company run to a cover set?

There are a number of solutions for weather-related problems that one can deal with in pre-production. In settling on a schedule, weather should be a primary concern. A wise production manager consults *Farmers Almanac* and gains a general sense of the weather in the area in which the company will shoot. Most locales have a rainy, dry, hot and cold season. If you want snow, avoid Louisiana. For dry conditions, stay away from Vancouver. New York City is ideal for shooting in the spring and fall, but summers and winters can be brutal because of the extreme temperatures. Of course Los Angeles has sunshine 360 days a year, in case you ever wondered why Hollywood resides on the left coast.

To control your luck a good rule of thumb when organizing the schedule is to shoot out (see glossary) exteriors. Once you are inside, whether it is a location or a sound stage, you are no longer at the mercy of the weather. Ideally you could make both options possible, like a bride scheduling her wedding outdoors, but hiring a chapel just in case. If your schedule affords you the choice to shoot out the exteriors, do so. Then if you run into inclement weather, the company has the option to shoot inside and not suffer any (or little) delay. If your schedule demands you shoot all interiors first, and then finish the filming outside, your company will then be dependent on the weather.

In addition to consulting *Farmers' Almanac*, the production manager should have a special radio tuned to the local airport, which constantly updates weather reports. This preparation can help you decide whether to shoot, not shoot, delay or run to interior sets with as much lead-time as possible. Rain calls are difficult to make, as weather reports are not always accurate. Will it really rain? If so, how much and for how long? Will it be a downpour? Will it last all day? Will it be intermittent? Once the company is on set for an exterior, you assess the weather, and then make a decision.

More often than not, a company can shoot around the rain, however difficult it is. Canceling a day's shoot is not an option. Grips can set up giant silks that act as umbrellas so the director can shoot tight material. Rain itself, especially fine rain or drizzle, does not show up on camera, unless it is backlit. People may get wet, but it is imperative one keeps the equipment dry. Wet lamps and power cables pose an electrical hazard and must be protected from the water at all times.

If possible, a director can place a cover set toward the end of the schedule. This is a set, always dressed, that can be used if the weather forces the company inside. Cover sets can be a luxury for a production, but they have allowed many a film to continue shooting when the weather turns sour.

If you *want* a rain or snow shoot, then by all means, take advantage of foul weather. But then Murphy's Law would dictate that you have the opposite problem — finding precipitation when you want it. And who knows how many beautiful scenes were written without snow, and then chance permitted the director to turn a weather problem into cinematic beauty? Truffaut said that the two most beautiful things on screen are a train and snow. This assumes a train in the snow would be the ultimate beauty shot.

There are other problems: What if you shoot a major snow scene, and then next day the snow melts? Having committed to a "snow" look you would have to either scrap the previous day's photography or make snow for the rest of the scene. Making snow and making rain is common in filmmaking, but it is expensive and time-consuming.

Rain machines can be turned on and off at will if the screenplay calls for a rain sequence. The same holds true for snow. Better a controlled environment than reliance on fickle weather. Nothing frustrates a director more than lack of control; Cocteau mused in his diary, "As soon as I was ready to shoot, it clouded over, a plane went by, a dog barked, guinea fowls drowned the actresses voices, or the sound went wrong."

A director strives for perfection every step of the way. Charlie Chaplin, upon completing principal photography for his classic film *The Gold Rush*, was dissatisfied with his leading lady's performance and reshot the entire film. "I wanted to put a hundred-piece orchestra on the scaffolding, playing sound-lessly. I was talked out of it," said Luis Buñuel. Martin Scorsese and Spike Lee have been known to go over schedule or tinker obsessively in the editing room to get their picture just right. But even the master makes compromises. Sidney Lumet recalls, "I once asked Akira Kurosawa why he had chosen to frame a shot in *Ran* in a particular way. His answer was that if he'd panned the camera one inch to the left, the Sony factory would be sitting there exposed, and if he'd panned an inch to the right, we would see the airport — neither of which belonged in a period movie."

Lumet adds that striving for perfection can only lead to heartburn because there are uncontrollable elements everywhere: "I'm dependent on weather, budget, what the leading lady had for breakfast, who the leading man is in love with." If directors realize 80 percent of their original plan or vision, they're doing well. With time and some clout, they can sometimes nudge that number over 80 percent, but 100 percent is unrealistic.

Making compromises doesn't have to mean you make a second-rate film. On the contrary, it can often improve the product. Jean Cocteau's beautiful film *Beauty and the Beast* was shot in France during World War II. Restrictions compelled Cocteau to abandon his fight to shoot in color, so he shot the film in black and white instead. Is the film less exciting? More exciting? It is what it is. And the passage of time has certainly shown the film to be a classic.

Almost every aspect of filmmaking requires compromise. The script may have to be altered; the number-one choice for the lead actress is unavailable; the director of photography is talented but slow; the budget doesn't stretch as far as originally intended; the schedule is blown out of the water by a severe storm; the director may have to direct despite a high fever; the pace of a scene doesn't match in dailies; the director loses patience and objectivity; all the luck is bad; the communications are poor; the command is not respected.

The areas in which a director needs to be particularly aware of potential compromise include schedule, location and personnel. A film is rarely shot in scene order, so the assistant director and director do their best to create a reasonable, responsible and efficient schedule. Whether working on a Movie Magic computer program, or a cardboard strip board, the key to scheduling is to balance fixed with flexible dates, and fixed with flexible locations. The schedule is still rough in early pre-production. Once the actors have been hired, it begins to solidify. (Actors have start and stop dates that form brackets around the schedule. Turnaround is addressed and factored into each day's photography. If an actor has a conflict, say a press junket for another film, these adjustments are made to the schedule.)

Locations are the next major factor to be added to the production board. Locations, particularly those slated for big and/or lengthy production scenes, may be available only at certain times or dates. Businesses, for example, are apt to be available only during off hours or after closing. Adjusting the production schedule to meld the schedule of the actors and the locations is a juggling act, one that can change in an instant. An actor becomes ill, a location falls out, and a scene goes over and must be stretched into the next day's principal photography. These things happen, and the director must deal with them.

The constant adjustment of the schedule can be frustrating to the director unaccustomed to compromise. A veteran is used to it. He has seen it all before.

Is it possible that there are no coincidences?
— M. Night Shyamalan

Sound on location can play havoc with a shoot. This is one reason why sound stages were invented: to avoid any compromise with the sound recording. A director tries to get good production sound. It is difficult to match sound quality and performance in an ADR (see glossary) session, months after the film has been shot. During the company walk-through of the location, the sound person will identify potential sound problems and act on them if possible. The humming of motors, such as refrigerators and air conditioning units, can be turned on and off during a take. There are, however, sounds that ring out beyond the reach of the production company authority. These include neighborhood dogs, wild animals, birds, trains, planes and automobiles. With unidirectional microphones, many sounds, such as traffic, can be eliminated or at least softened during the mix. A sharp noise, such as a dog bark or a car horn, however, can destroy a sound take.

One of the worst sounds a director contends with is that of low-flying airplanes. If the flight pattern of a small airport near a location can be diverted for the days of principal photography, a lot of headaches will be avoided. Directors, actors and the crew take a great deal of time to set up a shot. If a plane flies overhead, the director usually waits for it to pass before calling "action." If a plane buzzes in during a take, a director may stop the take, or continue, knowing the sound has been compromised. Stopping and starting for planes can become aggravating. Actor's concentration begins to slip. If the company is near an airport with planes regularly overhead, the director cannot wait each time a plane flies over, or the pages would never be made for the day. Therefore, directors can override the objections of the sound person and shoot take after take with the sound of the planes included. One director had the director of photography shoot some of the planes flying overhead and then incorporated them and their annoying sound into the story.

To address problems and to compromise as little as possible, the director has three remedies: money, script and invention. One reason why movies cost so much is that money can solve many problems. Many a production manager has sped over to a nearby airport and made a handsome offer to the flight controllers to reroute noisy planes. An angry shopkeeper claims the key grip broke the window on their shop. Money for a new window is produced immediately to placate the owner and avoid any potential conflicts.

Although many line budget items include healthy contingencies for unanticipated problems during principal photography, there is a limit. The next best thing to cash for a director is the script. Rather than go over budget or over schedule, the director has the power to adjust the screenplay to fit the circumstance. Remember that directors sign a contract that obliges them to shoot the story as written. This affords directors some leeway in altering the script, but in the end, they must deliver the story reflected in the screenplay. To change a comedy into a horror film, or an action film into a drama violates the trust instilled by the producers. In addition, the finished film must be a certain length. To cut pages and/or scenes to stay on schedule, which ultimately results in an unacceptable length, is a breach of contract.

But changes are always made: a complex scene can be simplified; a lengthy scene can be shortened; an expensive prop can be downgraded; a dialogue scene can be visualized rather than spoken; the 14-car train wreck can be heard off screen rather than shown. Think of the savings in both time and money!

Money shouldn't be the first solution; it should be the last. Necessity is the mother of invention. A director who needs to solve a problem becomes imaginative. Often a creative solution is organic to the story and more effective than throwing money at it. An entourage of horses can be replaced by a lone squire with a pair of coconuts, as was done in *Monty Python and the Holy Grail.* When Gilliam couldn't afford horses he opted for coconuts on screen to imply the clip-clop of horses. Very funny, very cheap and very Monty Pythonesque.

What could Cocteau have done about the barking dogs, the guinea fowl, and the sound machine? Unfortunately, very little. He could have sent a production assistant to the house with the dog to bribe the owner to keep Fideaux inside. He probably punted a lot. Like a general planning for battle, what looked great on paper can fly out the window once the first shots have been taken. Making adjustments because these changes of luck are one of the most exciting aspects of filmmaking. Who knows? Maybe it will even improve your product.

The moment just prior to shooting a scene is when the lines, business, props, set dressing, camera movement, lighting and interaction between actors and their environment are primed to create the shot. Though there has been an overall plan that organizes these elements to be prepared for this moment, a director should take a deep breath and allow the moment to materialize organically. This is where luck becomes a player. The history of filmmaking is rife with examples of what was perceived as bad luck turned into cinematic gold. When asked whether he really believed a horseshoe hanging over his door would bring his luck, Niels Bohr said, "Of course not, but I am told it works even if you don't believe in it." And golfer Gary Player wisely said, "The harder I work the luckier I get."

10

Chutzpah

*I'll snatch this story out of nothingness, by surprise tactics. And if fate's
against me I'll deal with fate. I'll cheat it with some card trick.*
— Jean Cocteau

Chutzpah is the element that binds the principles laid out in the previous nine chapters. Chutzpah is an intangible. It is hard to explain, difficult to acquire, yet essential to directing. This is what drives a director, separates the uninspired from the innovative, and provides armor to handle rejection. It is the passion to cling to an idea like a drowning sailor to a wooden plank. Chutzpah is utter nerve, guts, spunk, and gumption. Or as defined by Leo Rosten, "the quality enshrined in a man who, having killed his mother and father, throws himself on the mercy of the court as an orphan." Ultimately it smacks of courage. Courage, said Winston Churchill, is the greatest virtue; it makes all the others possible.

Too much chutzpah is obnoxious, too little may prove ineffectual. There is an extremely fine line between assertiveness and aggression. The proper amount of chutzpah reveals someone who is aggressively self-assured. In the shark-infested sea of show business, this quality can keep a director's head above water. The film industry is divided between those people whose job it is to say no and those who say yes. It is so much easier to say no. No to risk, no to uniqueness, no to new talent, no to experimentation. If an executive says no to a film that does wind up getting made and then flops, that executive is vindicated. And, in fact, more films flop than hit the jackpot. (I won't dwell on the fates of those who said no to *Star Wars*.)

Some brave souls must say yes or films wouldn't get made. Yes means

157

committing huge sums of money, yes means mustering large numbers of people, yes means possible unemployment for the yes-ee. One of the best reasons to say yes is finding a director who has unflagging passion for the project. For a producer to hand a production over to a director, the producer must be confidant in that director's ability to deliver.

According to the Director's Guild of America, fewer than 3 percent of its members are women. The rate is higher in Europe. Women have made great strides breaking the glass ceiling. There are many different types of films, and therefore plenty of opportunities for women directors. What it takes is chutzpah.

If there's specific resistance to women making movies, I just choose to ignore that as an obstacle for two reasons: I can't change my gender, and I refuse to stop making movies.
— Kathryn Bigelow

Although talent and passion make a great one-two punch, too many other factors contribute to a film's success to make any venture sure-fire. There is no formulae for success; or all films would hit their mark. But one can surely imagine the opposite. How would a producer feel about a project if the director committed by saying in a subdued tone, "Sure, why not?" or "Okay, I guess I can do it."

Chutzpah is an unspoken quality that makes everyone associated with the enterprise convinced this director, and only this director, is the anointed one. The director exudes passion that infects the company with confidence. This is the glue that will hold the company together, through thick and thin.

Akira Kurosawa once said, "I am a director ... that is all. I know myself well enough to know that if I ever lost my passion for films, then I myself would be lost. Film is what I am about." This total commitment to the craft, this unbridled enthusiasm, is gold to a producer. Directors with passion learn their dedication from an early age. Avid filmgoers, they get the bug by being transported by the works of both contemporary and classic directors. Others may call them foolish, but as Edgar Allan Poe once said, "I have great faith in fools — self-confidence my friends call it."

Terry Gilliam, said (when making *Brazil*), "Like most of my projects, I ended up wanting to do more than I was capable of doing." Directors constantly strive for excellence. They push themselves and the cast and crew who surround the picture. There is no room for mediocrity in cinema. The most serious crime in show business is to bore an audience. Alfred Hitchcock, in a 1947 press interview, said, "I aim to provide the public with beneficial shocks. Civilization has become so protective that we're no longer able to get our goose bumps instinctively. The only way to remove the numbness and revive our moral equilibrium is to use artificial means to bring about the shock. The best way to achieve that, it seems to me, is through a movie."

Sometimes it is necessary to push the material so as to shock the audience from their complacency. Once upon a time a character could be killed on screen by a single gunshot and no showing of blood. Then came color, then blood packs, then multiple blood packs, then spurting blood packs, and then slow motion spurting blood packs. Once a trend has been established, directors rarely go back to old ways. Instead, they build off the common practice and blaze new trails.

The assumed bravado of chutzpah is widespread in the industry. Luis Buñuel flaunted this trait when his film *The Discreet Charm of the Bourgeoisie* was nominated for an Oscar. Four Mexican reporters asked him if he thought he was going to win that Oscar. "Of course," he quipped. "I've already paid the $25,000 they wanted. Americans may have their weaknesses, but they do keep their promises." A few days later, headlines in Mexico City announced that Buñuel had bought the Oscar.

One would like to imagine that talent is all that it takes for success. Talent is a valuable thing, and it may be the key to longevity in the film business, but talent without assurance often withers on the vine. In real estate they say, "Location, location, location." In film it's "Persistence, persistence, persistence." Most people in the industry work a 60-hour week. Persistence can include hardship and stress. To have talent and wait by the phone will only get you a sore butt. To be a filmmaker one has to make film. Start and never stop. Some of the work will be good, some bad, some excellent, and some disappointing. It is the body of work that makes a filmmaker, not one movie.

Although many directors and actors are well paid for their services, money should be a minor factor in deciding whether or not to do a film. Luis Buñuel said it best, "As unlikely as it may sound, I've never been able to discuss the amount of money offered to me when I sign a contract. Either I accept or refuse, but I never argue. I don't think I've ever done something for money that I didn't want to do; and when I don't want to do something, no offer can change my mind. What I won't do for one dollar, I also won't do for a million."

Directors who break the mold, take risks and persist against over-whelming odds are said to have chutzpah. Eric Von Stroheim was only allowed to make nine silent films because of his extravagance, but they are some of the greatest films ever made. Fritz Lang was so far over budget on *Metropolis*, the production had to be shut down. He said, "The production company is invested so heavily in the film, they must finish it to make their money back." Lang merely waited until additional financing was raised. Kurosawa played the same waiting game on *The Seven Samurai*.

John Ford insisted on shooting his films on location in Monument Valley; Preston Sturges demanded to direct in exchange for selling his screenplays for a dollar; Francis Ford Coppola shot *The Godfather* in extremely low light; and Stanley Kubrick moved to England to distance himself from the studios.

A very talented director went to Paris to direct a play by Shake-speare, *Henry V*, at the famous Académie Française. The director had never directed a Shakespearian play before. With fear and trembling, he faced the incredibly well-trained and disciplined actors for the first rehearsal. The director looked into the determined faces of the actors, trained professionals familiar with drama, knowledgeable about Shake-speare. He knew if he admitted to these actors that he had never directed any Shakespeare, he would be not be able to gain their confidence and exercise the command necessary for the role of director. So he lied. He greeted the cast and announced that he had just come from Germany where he had successfully staged three of Shakespeare's history dramas, including the play scheduled for the Académie Française, *Henry V*. The actors then picked up their scripts and began the first read-through of what was to become a huge hit.

Conclusion

Can a film be made without a director? It's possible. Actors can direct themselves, the assistant director can call the shots, and the editor can stitch the scenes together. Just as a woodwind quartet plays without a conductor, a film could magically come to be by the sheer will of the participants.

In Paul Weiss's treatise on the nature of film art (Southern Illinois University Press, 1975), he offers: "Film that is dominated by a director is only one possible form of film. Film without any director, or film which shows no influence of a director, is film that is less than it ought to be. A good director makes sure that all the parts are creatively produced and brought together in a single totality.... He gains most when others are given their freedom to show what they know."

Elia Kazan maintains the director has to know everything. In addition to cameras, lenses, sound recorders, microphones, and mounts, the director should know literature, opera, acrobatics, painting, sculpture, dance, music, stage scenery, costuming, lighting, color, weather patterns, cities, plants, animals, oceans, topography, psychology, war, weapons, economics, food, current events, travel, sports, acting and him or herself.

In conclusion, these are some salient points one can take into the field as you prepare yourself to stand on the line and direct a film.

- Producing a film is a balance between a creative venture and fiscal responsibility. However, the actual making of the film is planned chaos. The money and resources allocated become the pallet, colors and canvas upon which the director paints the picture. The act of directing a film is so quixotic, invigorating and challenging, one must immerse one's whole being into the process. It is not for the faint of heart.

- Actors are trained in a variety of schools: Strasberg, Meisner, Weston, Restova, improv, classical and many more. The director must be aware of how each of the actors prefers to work. A method actor might need several takes to get up to speed, whereas an actor trained in improvisation might hit the right emotional marks on the first take.

- Filmmakers are trained to respect the 180-degree rule, to maintain eye-line, screen direction and continuity. There is no question it is better not to jump the line, to maintain proper screen direction and to preserve prop and wardrobe continuity whenever possible. But the history of cinema is chock full of screen direction and continuity errors, the vast majority of which go unnoticed. Remember, Walter Mirsch, in his book on editing titled *In the Blink of an Eye*, insists that continuity of action, clean matches and rhythm take a backseat to the overarching principle that the editor, like the screenwriter, actor, composer, and director, must do everything to follow the emotional arc of the story, even if it means sacrificing a clean cut for a highly charged, less clean one. He calls it being "true to the emotion of the moment."

- Filmmakers are taught the value of proper coverage. Like continuity, it is better to have excess coverage in the editing room rather than too little. But any director will tell you that in the battle to "chase the sun" and to "make the day," coverage is often simplified.

- An experienced director knows that the moments before calling "action" and those before shouting out "cut" are often used in the final film. The actor revving up energy just as the camera is about to roll, and the release of that tension at the conclusion of the take can make an impact on the shot, the scene and the movie. It takes so much effort to get to the moment of shooting that it is worth savoring it by delaying the "calls."

- The mantra "we'll fix it in post," often evoked to keep on schedule, can come back to haunt the director during the editing process. ADR and opticals, while part of film language, should be used sparingly.

- In the heyday of Hollywood, directors were under contract to churn out picture after picture. The producer often "finished" the film. Directors would shoot only enough coverage to make the film work. Everyone, the editor, producer, director, and studio chief, devoted themselves to making the best film possible. Giving a director final cut is a bit of a status symbol. It means a director has clout. But we see many examples of films these days that are bloated and over long because the director has lost all objectivity. On set the director is the only audience, yet the finished product is meant to be seen by as large an audience as possible. A director with final cut will bear this in mind.
- There are directors who out of either insecurity or ego do not listen to others in the day-to-day, minute-to-minute decision-making process. Filmmaking is a collaborative venture. A cast and crew that work in an environment open to the creative process will generate lots of ideas. The director sets this tone.
- A director requires an adequate budget to realize a film. Knowing how to interpret the needs of the script and put a proper price tag on it is one of the director's many responsibilities. But money comes with a price. The bigger the budget, the more the risk. The more the risk, the more controls by the financiers may be placed on the director.
- Although we learn from Kurosawa that films are talking — one talks though the script, talks through production, talks through the editing and then distribution — too much talk can be a distraction. Directors are hired to interpret a screenplay. They are expected to turn the words on the screenplay page into images. They can add a point of view or make a statement with their craft *if* it services the story. Directors, especially novice directors, tend to talk a lot about the process. A seasoned director learns that less is more on set. If the prep has been sufficient, most of the planning will have been accomplished and the shoot has the potential to go smoothly.
- A bizarre and/or interesting interpretation of a text is most successful when it permeates all aspects of the production. Let the work speak for itself. A director cannot stand before each audience and explain his or her interpretation.
- Actors dig deep into themselves to bring the life of a character to

the light of the screen. After long waits they are then asked to hit emotional marks during the short burst of a take. If the actors don't click, the film will suffer.

- Video tap is a crutch. It's a small television monitor that in no way simulates the effect an image or a shot will have on the big screen in a movie theater. The action is happening in the space between the actor and the lens. The director's energy is integral to that the process.
- When asked what material should be in a trailer, the director will ask for everything. In essence, they want a 100-minute trailer. It's too painful to cut anything out. Professional trailer editors look for trailer "moments," stark story points and exciting images. This is what teases an audience. Let them do their work.
- The director brings a certain energy and drive to the set. The shooting of the screenplay must be accomplished within the time allotted. Directors often complain that they do not have enough time. But while an extra hour or an extra day is welcome, too much additional time can be harmful. The pace is affected and, as has been stated in chapter 7, that change in pace will be reflected in the dailies. It would be wasteful. Time is not a commodity to be squandered.
- Storyboards are a valuable tool. By previsualizing the film, a director can walk onto the set with a plan on how to execute each day's work. But a plan devised on paper may not jive with the reality of the day. Locations are switched, set pieces changed, light may not always be controlled, actors performances develop and the director's own vision evolves. Pulling all the elements together to shoot a sequence is a Herculean task. The director must decide how to best compose the scene. The storyboards may indicate they are the best and most efficient way to shoot the scene. Or not.
- A film crew, like an army, moves on its stomach. To disregard issues related to food is a recipe for disaster. The craft services table is available to cast and crew all day. It is difficult to cater to the eating habits of the hundred people who make up the cast and crew. To demand the craft services table contain only health foods may be too extreme. But sugar, coffee, sodas and chips, when too readily available, may contribute to a blood sugar crash

and irritability. The attorney in the Harvey Milk murder trial used Twinkies as a defense.

- The director sees the whole picture. The actors are mainly concerned with performance and how they appear on screen. Allowing actors to attend dailies gives them an opportunity to worry about their look or even request reshoots. Best to leave these decisions to the director.
- It is easy for a director to have special feelings for a particular shot or sequence. The blood, sweat and tears that go into each shot can sometimes blind a director to its true relationship to the film. If, in the end, it does not service the film, it has to go. This is often referred to as "killing your children." This is why editors are not on set. Their task is to make a cohesive film in the editing room untainted by the chaotic nature of the production period.
- The director has the final say on set, but an order should not be given prematurely, especially one that will take time to undo. Laying tracks, painting walls, moving camera, changing lenses, or replacing lights all take time. Directors have the right to change their minds and order the tracks moved or the walls painted a different color, but the time lost will be time taken away from the production schedule. This is why pre-production, previsualization, and pre-planning can make or break a show.
- It is an interesting phenomenon that some actors can actually improve their performance in ADR. It is an important final touch by the actor on the quality of the film. While directors should avoid looping if possible (it is expensive and can be frustrating if the actor has difficulty dropping in lines), most films will require some ADR. If an actor is truly ADR challenged the director should consider re-editing the sequence to allow the actor to be off screen for the drop in lines. A really poor looping job can harm a scene. Some actor are so ADR challenged they have to drop in their lines one word at a time.

Basic Principles of Film Directing
- Clarify the chain of command to the crew
- Avoid duplication of energies
- Keep the ball rolling
- Keep bad news from the actors

- Avoid passing the buck
- Do not assume anything
- Delegate responsibility
- Double the time allotted for anything out of the ordinary
- Keep Murphy's Law in mind
- Stay healthy

In the simplest terms, directors come to the set, rehearse the actors, place the camera, wait for the set to be ready and then commence shooting. They call for action when the shot is lined up and cut the shot when the sequence is complete.*

This is repeated for each set-up and each scene called for in that day's production schedule. When the shooting day is over, the director goes to the laboratory to watch dailies with the department heads and the editor. Then home, bed and a night's rest.

Depending on whether it is a five- or six-day weekly schedule, the director has some time off during the weekend, but often that time is taken to prepare the following week's photography. To give you an idea of the shape of a shooting day, listen for the following phrases barked out (usually by the assistant director) over the din of the chaos:

- Quiet on the set!—This signifies the calm before the storm.
- Roll sound!—The sound recorder is activated.
- Roll camera!—The camera is turned on and is recording.
- Slate!—An electronic clapboard is placed in front of the lens to identify the shot. The clappers are snapped shut to mark the beginning of the scene and to create a digital time code to match sound and picture.
- Action!—The director signals for the actors to begin and/or for the camera to move.
- Cut!—The director signals for the actors and/or camera to stop.
- Check the gate!—This is to make sure the take was clean, that no dust or hairs got caught in the camera pressure plate.
- Back to one!—This signals a repeat of the shot.
- Camera moves!—When the shot is satisfactorily "in the can" the camera moves to the next position or "set-up."

*It is advisable to call for "action" only when the shot is primed. "Cut" should be called a few beats after the scene is finished, for, while the actors are still in character, sometimes a little magic happens of which editors often make use.

- Martini shot!—The last shot of the day.
- That's a wrap!—Principal photography for the day ends.

The directing of a picture involves coming out of your individual lone-liness and taking a controlling part in putting together a small world. A picture is made. You put a frame around it and move on. And one day you die. That is all there is to it.

—John Huston

This is the job of a director. It is up to each individual to interpret the script, excite the actors, create dynamic visuals and a heart-pounding pace. The fundamentals outlined in this book are tested and valuable. But rules are often made to be broken. Bend the rules; smash convention. I leave you with Billy Wilder's wise words about directing: "I have ten commandments. The first nine are, thou shalt not bore. The tenth is, thou shalt have the right of final cut."

Appendix: Film vs. Digital

Revolution is not a onetime event.
— Audre Lorde

Revolution is quick change; evolution is slow change. As much as we feel the pressure of the digital rage, it is but one of many revolutions in the on-going technological evolution. In our fever to keep up, we often forget that this revolution is being fueled by wholesalers' marketing schemes to coerce sales.

We have seen the CD-ROM world and the Dot COM world, both part of this digital grail, fall without grace into a sea of despair. They were quickly replaced by the next wave of technologies; RED, iTunes, YouTube, etc., and there has been no looking back. But what concerns me most, as a member of the film community, is that revolutions compel individuals to take sides. "I'm digital, new technology, zeros and ones rule!" or "The look of film is bee-u-tee-ful." We're engaged in a battle over whether to go completely digital or retain the film medium.

Movies are meant to be seen. And currently, the standard for capturing and projecting movies internationally is via film. I do not have a crystal ball. I cannot say when digital technology will replace film. All signs point that way, but I for one believe that the road to that inevitability is longer than we think. Certainly longer than the digital manufacturing industry thinks.

I like computers. I like the digital arena ... for some things. Word processing, games, Internet surfing, research and nonlinear editing. Where I am cautious is in image capture and distribution. While the general public cannot tell the difference between a film shot or projected on stock or digital, I can. The argument that digital image capture is inexpensive and as a result a director can shoot a lot of material is countered by the fact there are only so many hours in a day in which to make the pages. Light, shadows and color read much better on film. Granted, there are situations in which shooting high def makes sense, especially on an actor-driven project, but if one is going to put up millions of dollars to gather a top-notch cast and crew to shoot a terrific script, why not use film? The expenses related to high def shooting, especially in the enhancement process during post-production, make the medium less of a bargain than one might expect.

If a film or digital project is made up of four equally divided stages, pre-production, production, post-production and distribution, we can safely say that digital technology dominates one of these areas — post-production. It took ten years, and now editing on film has become extinct. But how many filmmakers now have not one, not two, but several versions of their story on hard drives? The ability to shoot 30-to-1 or 50-to-1 is more of a problem than a benefit. What that tells me is knowing the facility of digital technology was available, forethought, that means working out the kinks in the story, was given short shrift. Now the filmmakers find themselves in post-production without having fulfilled some of the pre-production requirements ... getting the story.

Digital technology has made inroads into pre-production with screenplay formatting, storyboarding programs and effective budgeting and scheduling software. No computer has yet to write a good screenplay or cast a film.

In production and distribution, digital technology is now making effective inroads. Some films have been shot in high def digital, and some have been projected on digital projectors. But these are not yet industry standard. Most films are shot and projected on 35mm and will be for a while. Even though digital projection is currently available, without a business model to change all movie theaters over from 35mm film to digital projection, at a cost of more than $150,000 per theater, film prints still need to be struck. Distributors and exhibitors are still struggling over who should pay for this expense.

To quote well-known cinematographer John Bailey, film has changed format once in 100 years, whereas video has changed 50 times in that many years. Kodak predicts they will continue to manufacture 35mm, 16mm and even 8mm stock for the next 20 years. When a new technology first enters the marketplace, bells from all quarters are sounded; attention is paid; people sign on quickly. And technology has encroached on the film business rapidly.

But, though this revolution is still being waged, there will be another, perhaps even more seductive, revolution to follow ... and another ... and another. And that is what evolution is all about.

A negative is a physical entity. It lasts over 50 years, and the new stocks may last hundreds of years. A digital project resides on a server. And with watermarking, password protection and encryption technology still being researched, I feel my concerns about copyright are genuine. The U.S. Library of Congress insists on 35mm film as the best means to preserve our moving image national heritage. Starting in the 1950s, the Library began to re-photograph paper prints to convert them back into films again, initially onto 16mm film and then onto 35mm film. The digital preservation project initiated in the 1990s has been impetus to make more 35mm prints of national works in order to have a superior digital image from which to work. The Academy of Motion Picture Arts and Sciences concluded a study in 2007 that it costs $1,200 per year over 10 years to archive and preserve a 35mm negative verses $12,000 per year over 10 years to archive a digital master feature. That is 10 times the cost for protecting a digital library.

Digital video project resides on a server. With 17-year-old boys in Norway cracking the MPAA DVD codes, and watermarking and password protection still being researched, I feel my concerns about copyright are genuine.

Glossary

above-the-line: The part of a production budget earmarked for the creative aspects of production, including the salaries of the producer, director, writer, and talent.

AD: *See* assistant director.

ADR: *See* automatic dialogue replacement.

agent/talent agent: An individual or company licensed by the state to represent a particular talent in the entertainment field and to seek employment and negotiate contracts on his or her behalf. The standard fee is 10 percent of the client's salary. Agents can represent above-the-line talent (actors, writers, directors, producers) or below-the-line talent (art directors, directors of photography, editors).

ambient noise: (1) Background noise. (2) A sound occurring naturally in a location.

angle: With reference to the subject, the direction from which a picture is taken — that is, the camera-subject relationship.

aspect ratio: The ratio of picture width to height, such as 1.33:1 (16mm), 1.85:1 (35mm), or 2.35:1 (70mm).

assistant director (AD): The person who helps the production manager break down the script during pre-production and keeps the director on schedule during production. The AD also hires, controls, and directs background action, including extras and camera vehicles.

auteur theory: Truffaut claimed that film, ideally, is a medium of personal expression for the director, whom, for that reason, was to be regarded as an *auteur*.

automatic dialogue replacement (ADR): A process during post-production in which an actor replaces any of his or her lines in the film that were not recorded properly during production.

beat: (1) The point in a scene where a character's tempo, meaning, or intention shifts. (2) A musical tempo used for timing motion picture action.

below-the-line: The part of a production budget allocated to the technical aspects of production, including the salaries of the crew and equipment and material costs.

blocking: How the director positions the actors and the camera on the stage or set.

boom: A support pole, held by a boom operator, used to hang the microphone close to the performers but just out of the shot.

bounce light: Light that is reflected off white cards, ceilings, or walls to illuminate a subject indirectly.

breakdown sheet: A list made from a script that includes all elements needed to produce a sequence.

business: Activity invented by actors to identify their characters' behavior. Business is a physical action that arises from dialogue, silences or pauses, or audio cues (such as a doorbell or ringing phone). It might involve movement from one part of the set to another (crosses) or the use of props and set dressing. Examples: lighting a cigarette at a key moment in a scene or jiggling a set of keys to break a tense silence.

"C" (century) stand: A metal stand with legs and brackets designed to hold flags that block and shape the light.

call back: To ask actors to audition for a second or third time.

camera axis: A hypothetical line running through the optic center of the camera lens.

camera operator: The person who operates the camera. This person might also be the director of photography.

character: A person portrayed in an artistic piece, such as a drama or novel.

close-up (CU): A tight shot of an object or an actor's face and shoulders.

closed set: When the environment in which principle photography is taking place is populated with only the essential cast and crew personnel

cookie (kukaloris): A thin panel with regular or irregular shapes cut out, permitting light directed through it to form a particular arrangement on a part of the set.

completion bond: The insurance brokerage firm that guarantees to the investors the film will be made or their money returned.

composition: (1) The arrangement of artistic parts to form a unified whole. (2) The balance and general relationship of objects and light in the frame.

contingency fund: A sum of money, approximately 10 percent of the budget, that is added to the overall production budget in case of cost overruns and production problems.

continuity: The smooth flow of action or events from one shot or sequence to the next.

continuity script: A script made for post-production by the script supervisor. A continuity script contains a shot-by-shot account of the contents of the film.

costume designer: The person who designs and supervises the making of garments for the actors.

cover set: A predressed location available in case inclement weather forces the company to move indoors.

coverage: The different angles from which a particular scene is shot.

craft services: The person or persons responsible for feeding the crew.

crane: A boom that supports the camera and can be raised or lowered during the shot.

cutaway: A shot of an object or a view that takes viewers away from the main action.

dailies: Picture and sound work prints of a day's shooting, usually an untimed one-light print, made without regard to color balance.

day out of days: A detailed schedule of the days the actors will work on a film production.

deal memo: A letter between two parties that defines the basic payment and responsibility clauses and the spirit of what will later become a contract.

director: The person who interprets the written book or script and oversees all aspects of a film production.

director of photography (DP): In production, the person who directs the cinematography (the lighting and camera setup and framing).

distributor: A company that sells, leases, and rents films.

dolly: (1) A truck built to carry a camera and camera operator to facilitate movement of the camera during the shooting of scenes. (2) To move the camera toward or away from the subject while shooting a scene.

DP: *See* director of photography.

dress rehearsal: The final rehearsal or technical drill for a production before actual filming. A dress rehearsal involves costumes, props, and dressed sets.

editing: The process of selecting the shots and sequences that will be included in the final product, their length, and the order in which they will appear.

editor: The person who decides which scenes and takes are to be used, how, where, in what sequence, and at what length they will appear.

establishing shot: A shot that establishes a scene's geographical and human contents.

exposure: The amount of light that acts on a photographic material. Exposure is the product of illumination intensity (controlled by the lens opening) and duration (controlled by the shutter opening and the frame rate).

eye-line: The line from an actor's eye to the direction in which the actor is looking. If the actor looks at co-performers and behind them is an audience, the actor might become distracted. It is important to keep crew members out of an actor's eye-line during auditions and principal photography.

final cut: The last editing of a work print before conforming is done and before sound work prints are mixed.

floor plan: A scale drawing of a location that is used to plan lighting, camera, and actor blocking.

focus: To adjust a lens so that it produces the sharpest visual image on a screen, on a camera film plane, and so on.

foley: Sound effects made by a foley artist who matches sounds made by the actors such as footsteps, rug beating, head scratching, etc.

foreground: The part of the scene in front of the camera that is occupied by the object nearest to the camera.

genre: A category of film categorized by a particular style, form, or content, such as horror, sitcom, Western, and domestic drama.

golden time: A rate of pay equal to triple the base hourly wage.

green room: A comfortable holding area for the actors.

grip: A person who performs a variety of tasks during film production, including helping to set up cameras, lighting equipment, and sets.

gross profit: Total, aggregate, as in gross national product.

headroom: Compositional space in a shot above the actor's head.

high-hat: A tripod head mounted onto a flat board. This allows the cameraman to place the camera on the ground or on a table for a low-angle shot.

highlights: The brightest areas of a subject. In a negative image, highlights are the areas of greatest density; in a positive image, they are the areas of least density.

insert: A close shot of detail.

intensity (light): The total visible radiation produced by a light source. The term refers to the power (strength) of the light source.

key light: The main illumination of the subject.

key-to-fill ratio: *See* lighting ratio.

kicker: A separation light placed directly opposite the key light to create side and back light.

laboratory: A facility that processes and prints film and sometimes offers additional services, such as coding, negative cutting, editing, and film storage.

lens: (1) A ground or molded piece of glass, plastic, or other transparent material with opposite surfaces, either or both of which are curved, by means of which light rays are refracted so that they converge or diverge to form an image. (2) A combination of two or more such pieces, sometimes with other optical devices like prisms, used to form an image for viewing or photographing. Also called *compound lens*.

lighting director: In film production, the person who designs and supervises the lighting setup.

lighting ratio: The ratio of the intensity of key and fill lights to fill light alone.

line item: A budget entry.

lined script: A script marked by the script supervisor to show the editor which take number was used to record each part of all scenes.

long shot (LS): The photographing of a scene or action from a distance or with a wide angle of view so that a large area of the setting appears on the film and the scene or objects appear quite small.

looping: The process of lip-sync dubbing.

low-key: A lighting style that uses intermittent pools of light and darkness with few highlights and many shadows. The contrast is created by a high ratio of key light alone to key and fill lights.

LS: *See* long shot.

magic hour: This is the time between sundown and darkness when the quality of light has an especially "magic" or warm quality — twilight.

master shot: Usually a long shot in which all action in a scene takes place. Action is repeated for the medium shot and close-up, which may be cut into the same scene.

match cut: A cut made between two different angles of the same action using the subject's movement as the transition.

matte: An opaque outline that limits the exposed area of a picture, either as a cutout object in front of the camera or as a silhouette on another strip of film.

meal penalties: A fine levied against the production to pay additional money to actors who were not allowed to eat at the prescribed break time.

medium shot: A scene that is photographed from a medium distance so that the full figure of the subject fills an entire frame.

mise-en-scène: The totality of lighting, blocking, camera use, and composition that produces the dramatic image on film.

mix: To combine the various sound tracks — dialogue, music, and sound effects — into a single track.

mix cue sheet: A list of all dialogue, effects, and music cues for a sound mix. Mix cue sheets are organized sequentially for each sound track.

mixer: (1) Circuitry capable of mixing two or more sound inputs to one output. (2) The audio console at which mixing is done. (3) The person who does the mixing.

Murphy's Law: The observation that "anything that can go wrong will go wrong."

narration: The off-screen commentary for a film. Also known as *voice-over (VO)*.

negative cost: The amount of money required to complete the film.

net points: The percentage of the net profit.

net profit: Profit remaining after all deductions have been made.

on-screen sound: A sound emanating from a source that is visible within the frame.

180°-axis-of-action rule: A means of camera placement that ensures continuity and consistency in the placement and movement of objects from shot to shot.

optical: Any visual device, such as a fade, dissolve, wipe, iris wipe, ripple dissolve, matte, or superimposition prepared with an optical printer in a laboratory or online for video.

over-the-shoulder shot: A shot in which a camera is placed behind and to the side of an actor, so that the actor's shoulder appears in the foreground and the face or body of another appears in the background. This type of shot tends to establish a specific subject's physical point of view on the action.

overtime: Additional salary that is paid if someone is asked to work longer than his or her contracted hours.

PA: *See* production assistant.

pace: A subjective impression of the speed of the sounds or visuals.

pan: A camera move in which the camera on a fluid head appears to move horizontally or vertically, usually to follow the action or to scan a scene. In animation, the effect is achieved by moving the artwork under the camera.

perspective: The technique of representing three-dimensional objects and depth relationships on a two-dimensional surface.

playback: Previously recorded music or vocals to be used on the set for the actors to perform to or mime. Playback is used when filming songs (music videos), instrumental performances, or dance.

point-of-view (POV) shot: A shot in which the camera is placed in the approximate position of a specific character. It is often preceded by a shot of a character looking in a particular direction and is followed by a shot of the character's reaction to what he or she has seen. The latter shot is sometimes called a *reaction shot*.

POV shot: *See* point-of-view shot.

practical light: A source lighting instrument on the set, such as a floor or table lamp, that appears in the frame.

prerig: To set up the lighting instruments based on a lighting plan devised by the director of photography a day or two before the shoot date. Prerigging can be done by a "swing crew" the night before the shoot.

presence: A recorded sound track from the location used to fill sound gaps in editing.

product placement: A relationship between the production company and a manufacturer to use a product in the film in exchange for a credit. The product is then donated to the film.

production assistant: An inexperienced crew member who floats from department to department, depending on which area needs help the most. Duties can range from running for coffee or holding parking spaces to setting up lights and slating.

production supervisor: An assistant to the producer. The production supervisor is in charge of routine administrative duties.

prosthetic makeup: Makeup and latex pieces designed to transform the appearance of a performer's face or body. Examples: a long nose for Cyrano or stitches and a big head for Frankenstein's creature.

quote: The most recent fee paid to a cast or crew member.

rack focus: A focus that shifts between foreground and background during a shot to prompt or accommodate an attention shift (a figure enters a door at the back of the room, for instance).

raw stock: Unexposed and unprocessed motion picture film, including camera original, laboratory intermediate, duplicating, and release-print stocks.

reaction shot: A close-up of a character's reaction to events.

reflected light: Light that has been bounced or reflected from objects, as opposed to direct or incident light.

reflected reading: A light meter reading of the intensity of light reflected by the subject and/or background.

reflector: Any surface that reflects light.

release: A statement giving permission to use an actor's face or likeness. It also releases a producer from future legal action, such as for slander or libel, which is signed by people appearing in a video program or film who are not professional performers.

residuals: A payment made to a performer, writer, or director for each repeat showing of a recorded television show or commercial.

reticle: A scale on transparent material (as in an optical instrument) used especially for measuring or aiming.

room tone: The natural acoustical ambiance of the area around which the scene is shot. Room tone can later be mixed with the dialogue to smooth cuts and create a more realistic presence of a space.

rough cut: A preliminary stage in film editing in which shots, scenes, and sequences are laid out in the correct approximate order, without detailed attention to the individual cutting points.

royalty fees: Money paid to composers, authors, performers, and so on, for the use of copyrighted materials.

rushes: Unedited raw footage as it appears after shooting.

SAG: The acronym for the Screen Actors Guild. The SAG contract also covers members of Equity (stage actors), AGVA (variety members), and AFTRA (television actors).

scale: The base union wage.

score: Music composed for a specific film.

script supervisor: The person who maintains the continuity in performer actions and prop placements from shot to shot and who ensures that every scene in the script has been recorded.

setup: The combination of lens, camera placement, and composition to produce a particular shot.

SFX: *See* sound effects.

shoot out: To group together and complete all photography with a specific, usually big ticket, element, such as an expensive actor, crowd scenes, and night scenes.

shooting ratio: The ratio of the material recorded during production to that which is actually used in the final edited version.

shooting script: The approved final version of the script with scene numbers, camera setups, and other instructions by the director.

shot: An unbroken filmed segment; the basic component of a scene.

silhouette: An outline that appears dark against a light background.

slow burn: A gradually increasing sense or show of anger.

soft cut: A very short dissolve.

soft light: Light made up of soft, scattered rays resulting in soft, less clearly defined shadows. Also known as *diffuse light.*

sound effects (SFX): Any sound from any source other than the tracks bearing synchronized dialogue, narration, or music. The sound effects track is commonly introduced into a master track during rerecording, usually with the idea of enhancing the illusion of reality in the finished presentation.

staging: The process of planning how the action of a scene will take place.

stand-in: Someone who takes the place of an actor during setup or for shots that involve special skills, such as horse riding or fight scenes.

stop date: A date specified in an actor's contract at which time they must be free to move on to another engagement.

storyboard: Semi detailed drawings of what each shot will look like, similar to a multipanel cartoon.

stripboard: A scheduling device. Each shot is represented by a strip of cardboard on which is encoded all the pertinent breakdown information. The strips are put in the desired order of shooting and are affixed to a multipanel stripboard. This board can then be carried to the set in the event that adjustments need to be made in the schedule.

swing crew: A team of gaffers or grips that sets the stage, lights, or both for a big or complicated sequence before the main production unit arrives.

take: A photographic record of each repetition of a scene. A particular scene might be photographed more than once in an effort to get a perfect recording of some special action.

theme: (1) A central concept, idea, or symbolic meaning in a story. (2) A repeated melody in a symphony or long musical composition.

turnaround: The time between ending one day's work and beginning the next day's.

TV safe: The innermost frame outline in the viewfinder, or the area that will be seen when screened on a television monitor. Elements outside this frame line may be missed. *See* reticle.

vaudeville: Vaudeville began as burlesque, using spectacular scenery, beautiful women, music and comedy to attract large, predominantly male, audiences. Early in the century, burlesque began to be transformed into modern vaudeville, which would appeal more to the family audience.

video assist: A video camera attached to a film camera for instant dailies, allowing the shot to be immediately judged on playback. Also known as *video tap*.

video tap: *See* video assist.

viewfinder: An eyepiece or screen through which a camera operator sees the image being recorded. *See* reticle.

visualization: The creative process of transforming a script into a sequence of visual images and sounds.

VO: Voice-over. *See* narration.

wrangler: An animal trainer and supervisor.

wrap: The period at the end of a day of shooting during which the crew must store the equipment.

Bibliography

Directing

Buñuel, Luis. *My Last Breath*. London: Fontana Paperbacks, 1982.
Cocteau, Jean. *La Belle et la bête: Journal d'un film*. Iuniverse, 1999
Clurman, Harold. *On Directing*. New York: Macmillan, 1974.
Jung, Carl. *Man and His Symbols*. New York: Dell, 1968
Kurosawa, Akira. *Something Like an Autobiography*. New York: Vintage, 1983.
Mamet, David. *On Directing*. New York: Viking, 1991.
Miller, Pat P. *Script Supervision and Film Continuity*, 2d ed. Boston: Focal, 1990.
Rabiger, Michael. *Directing: Film Techniques and Aesthetics*. Boston: Focal, 1989
Stanislauski, Constantin. *An Actor Prepares*. New York: Theater Arts, 1948.
_____. *Building a Character*. New York: Theater Arts, 1981.
Truffaut, François. *Hitchcock*. New York: Simon & Schuster, 1967.

The Industry

Behlmer, Rudy, ed. *Memo from David O. Selznick*. New York: Viking, 1972.
Eaker, Sherry, ed. *The Back Stage Handbook for Performing Artists*. Rev. and enlarged ed. New York: Watson-Guptill, Back Stage Books, 1991.
Litwak, Mark. *Reel Power*. New York: William Morrow, 1986.
Mayer, Michael F. *The Film Industries: Practical Business/Legal Problems in Production, Distribution and Exhibition*. New York: Hastings House, 1978.
Vogel, Harold L. *Entertainment Industry Economics*. New York: Cambridge University Press, 1986.

Production

Goodell, Gregory. *Independent Feature Film Production: A Complete Guide from Concept through Distribution*. New York: St. Martin's, 1982.
Gregory, Mollie. *Making Films Your Business*. New York: Schocken Books, 1979.

Irving, David K., and Peter W. Rea. *Producing and Directing the Short Film and Video*. Boston: Focal, 1996.
Singleton, Ralph S. *Film Scheduling: Or, How Long Will It Take to Shoot Your Movie?* 2d ed. Los Angeles: Lone Eagle, 1991.

Writing

Field, Syd. *The Foundations of Screenwriting*. New York: Dell, 1982.
Goldman, William. *Adventures in the Screen Trade*. New York: Warner Books, 1984.
McKee, Robert. *Story: Substance, Structure, Style and the Principles of Screenwriting*. New York: HarperCollins, 1997
Strunk, White and Osgood. *The Elements of Style*. New York: Macmillan, 1959

Periodicals/Newsletters

Cinéfantastique. 7240 W. Roosevelt Road, Forest Park, IL 60130: (708) 366-5566.
Variety (daily or weekly). 5700 Wilshire Boulevard, Suite 120, Los Angeles, CA 90036: (213) 857-6600; or 249 W. 17th Street, 4th Floor, New York, NY 10011: (212) 645-0067.

Index

183